BAD ECONOMICS

Pestilent Economists, Profligate Governments, Debt, Dependency & Despair

PETER SMITH

For my Dad

I would like to thank my wife Amanda for encouraging me to persevere and for her insightful comments on a formative draft. I would like to thank Keith Windschuttle who, as editor of Quadrant, *gave me the opportunity to have a number of articles published which have informed, and are reflected in, parts of this book; and Michael Connor, editor of* Quadrant Online, *for his perceptive comments on just a short excerpt from what I had thought was a final draft, which led me to a painful but valuable rewriting. Finally, I would like to thank my good friend Steven Kates, who has taken on his shoulders in Australia the task of exposing the nonsense that is Keynesian economics and whose knowledge and wisdom, in many shared conversations, over many years, have informed and sharpened my own views. All are absolved from responsibility for the content which hopefully will find some people nodding in agreement while undoubtedly irritating others. C'est la vie. Such is the politically divided state of the world in which we live.*

Published in 2012 by Connor Court Publishing Pty Ltd

Copyright © Peter Smith 2012

ALL RIGHTS RESERVED. This book contains material protected under International and Federal Copyright Laws and Treaties. Any unauthorized reprint or use of this material is prohibited. No part of this book may be reproduced or transmitted in any form or by any means, electronic or mechanical, including photocopying, recording, or by any information storage and retrieval system without express written permission from the publisher.

Connor Court Publishing Pty Ltd.
PO Box 1
Ballan VIC 3342
sales@connorcourt.com
www.connorcourt.com

ISBN: 9781921421594 (pbk.)

Cover design by Ian James

Printed in Australia

TABLE OF CONTENTS

Prologue...1
Preface..3
1: The Key to Truth...7
2: Prices and Prosperity..15
3: Saving and Investing..23
4: Keynes and Keynesians..29
5: Keynesian World...37
6: Pre-Keynesian World..47
7: Booming and Busting...61
8: Holy Holes in the Economy! The GFC............................79
9: Holy Holes II: Woeful Policy...99
10: Holy Holes III: Pestilent Economists...........................105
11: Dressed up Statistical Nonsense..................................113
12: Contradiction in Terms...121
13: Spreading the Wealth...139
14: Hope and Despair...157
15: Cargo Cult and Dependency..165
16: International Aid and Migration..................................173
17: Unhinged from Practicality..183
18: Utopia...187
19: Bad Arithmetic..193
20: Masters of the Economic Universe..............................197
21: Grand Bargain...201
Appendix: Temperamental Bias..215
Index..229

Prologue

Debt, dependency and unemployment scar the landscape of almost every Western nation. What has happened? Bad economics has happened; and increasingly burdensome and intrusive government.

Let there be no mistake; no wimping out and sharing the blame. Free market capitalism is not the problem. It is not even a miniscule part of the problem. Bad economics and government is the problem. It is the only problem.

Since Roosevelt's New Deal formed a destructive alliance with the simplistic economics of John Maynard Keynes, governments have borrowed and spent without care bequeathing economic morbidities and food stamp fare. And yet still they are looked to by an overwhelming number of people to provide the answers to life's problems.

Governments and their economists have led us down a ruinous road. Economics properly understood (good economics) is the guide to recovery. Good economics lays out how individual efforts and talents make societies prosperous. It is a credo of hope. The despair in Western societies caused by suffocating government debt, endemic unemployment and debilitating dependency on the nanny state is the product of embracing another credo that masquerades as economics. In fact, it is socialism to varying extents and in various guises. While it is still far from the stultifying socialism of post-war Eastern Europe, it is creeping insidiously into Western societies. Its proponents often put a "progressive" label on it. This is apt because it progressively robs people of their independence and self-reliance. It is immoral. It stunts people's growth, notwithstanding the sanctimony of its proponents.

Creeping socialism is nourished by the conviction that free market outcomes need continual and massive correction. It has no faith in capitalism or in individuals. Its faith is in the power of governments to steer societies collectively towards nirvana. Its legitimacy is bolstered by a claimed exclusive lien on compassion. Keynesian economics has become its most potent "scientific" prop. It is all a house of cards. None of it survives proper economic scrutiny.

Capitalism is enormously resilient and accommodative. It takes a long time and a great deal of bad economics and intrusive government to bring the current magnitude of economic malaise. From here it can get worse. It is time to start undoing the harm before economic malaise turns into social unrest of convulsive proportions and the potential loss of our freedoms.

Preface

Economic myths are abroad. People who have never studied one word of economics pronounce on the need to get consumers spending or agree that government has responsibility to stimulate the economy and create jobs. It is all the insidious product of the purveyors of bad economics. Who are they? They are called economists. Not all economists of course; just most of them.

In this book, the disingenuous is dumped and a clear path is hewn through some big picture economics – without complexity, diagrams or formulas – and through a number of left/progressive myths and pipedreams. It is polemical in style. No economics is required. It is written for a general readership. At the same time, social science students (doing economics or politics) may benefit from it; particularly those facing, or enduring, indoctrination in a typically progressive university setting. A cautionary note is necessary. Those on the confirmed left of the political spectrum are unlikely to find it comprehensible. They do believe, without question or doubt, that big government is the answer to life's problems.

Prosperity in Western societies is not a mystery. Free market capitalism explains it. Economics lays it bare. Chapter 1 provides a working definition of economics prefaced by a brief personal story of my own insight into the value of economics in uncovering the truth. Chapters 2 and 3 explain the role of those building blocks of prosperity: free market prices, and private-sector saving and investing. I am sorry to say that they are a little didactic. However, they have the virtue of brevity and provide the essential groundwork for understanding why Keynesian economics and government interference in market processes are misconceived.

John Maynard Keynes is the most famous and influential economist of the 20th century. Unfortunately, to put it extremely kindly, he had a flawed appreciation of capitalism. This has been costly. Keynesian economists have predominated in advising Western governments since the end of the Second World War. As a result, Western societies are less prosperous than they would otherwise have been and more deeply mired in the misery of debt and dependency. Fondly embraced by those on the left of the political spectrum, Keynesian economics has given theoretical backing to government intervention to counter capitalism's perceived shortfalls. It has relegated the critical role of market prices to a footnote and made a vice out of the virtue of saving.

Keynesian economics is explained in Chapters 4 to 6 where it is shown to be a misguided, simplistic and damaging replacement for the economics that it supplanted. The question is posed: was Keynes, despite his glittering career and reputation, an economic "crackpot", mistakenly given the cloak of genius.

Chapters 7 to 11 put Keynesian economics into the context of economic cycles; and what can and can't be done about them; and what should and shouldn't be done about them. The last major economic downturn, the Global Financial Crisis (GFC), and its aftermath, are explored as a backdrop to showing the puerile (yet resilient) nature of Keynesianism. Because of its severity, the GFC caused wholesale rethinking about the appropriate role of government in economic and financial affairs. Unsurprisingly, as most of economics profession and governments were followers of Keynesian economics, that rethinking was either misguided at best or plain silly at worst. If you are hijacked by a wrongheaded economic theory (by Keynesian quackery) it is not surprising that you implement wrongheaded policies. I show that Keynesian economics is buttressed by a tendentious use of statistics that allows governments and their economists to "prove" that they are right whatever the course of events.

Chapters 12 and 13 broaden the economics picture beyond economic cycles to the incompatibility of socialism and economics; and to the flawed economic arguments which infect the debate about the distribution of income and wealth.

Keynesian economics has become part of a more general interventionist economic agenda. This agenda is based on the misconception that free markets have to be corrected and moulded by government. It finds a receptive home among those on the left of the political spectrum. It has become part of their worldview. Chapter 14 shows how this agenda is at odds with good economics, is full of myths and specious arguments, and brings despair and impoverishment against the hope and prosperity that self-reliance and free markets bring.

Extending the theme of Chapter 14, Chapters 15 and 16 consider the damaging culture of dependency that is engendered by progressive thinking in both domestic and international settings.

The question arises: why does a culture of entitlement and dependency hold sway among so many when it patently does so much damage. I don't know the answer of course. I have an appendix which hypothesises a sociological explanation but this is a shot in the dark and should be regarded as no more. What seems to be clear is that the progressive economic agenda is disconnected from the strictures of practicality. Being loosed from practicality allows error and misconception to lurk. Dismal experience is put into the perspective of a golden age that can be achieved if only collectively we get it right. This progressive phenomenon of being unhinged from practicality; of making utopian pledges; of bad arithmetic; and of having delusions of power over economic events, is explored in chapters 17 to 20.

In the final Chapter (Ch. 21) it is suggested that the global debt crisis among Western governments; the resultant push back against Keynesianism, and the growing appreciation of the need to pare back the size of government and entitlements, offer hope in an otherwise dismal prognosis. A grand bargain is proposed between those on the industrial left and conservatives as a way to begin finding a lasting fix for Western economies.

6

1
The Key to Truth

The correctness of a statement cannot, the method [of Socrates] suggests, be determined by whether it is held by the majority or has been believed for a long time by important people.
Alain De Botton *(Consolations of Philosophy,* Penguin, 2000)

My dad was a motor mechanic for the local ambulance service in Liverpool, England. He voted for the British Labour Party. Though not active as a trade unionist he was politically-minded and often discussed politics at home. Two of these discussions now form an important part of my appreciation of economics, and its capacity, when properly understood, to clear away the fog and aid clear thinking.

Illusions and Delusions

Dad was talking to one of my uncles about a conversation he'd had with my maternal grandmother. She had always voted Tory and queried dad's support for the Labour Party. He was explaining to her why he voted for the Labour Party, when she interrupted, "but Bob the Labour Party people haven't any money to run the country". Labour Party people wore cloth caps in those days not Savile Row suits. He tried to explain, apparently without complete success, that politicians didn't use their own money in running the country. They used taxpayers' money.

That it is taxpayers' money is still usually buried in the subtext when governments explain how they intend to spend money. Perhaps my grandmother was simply taking governments at their word in forming her idiosyncratic view. I will come back to this story further on. It resonates still as a commentary on the grandiose way governments comport themselves; *dispensing treasure and holding kingly sway.*

On another occasion, when the topic had turned to the plight of the poor, probably because of some television program, my older sister Marjorie asked why the government could not just print more money and give it to poor people. While this seemed an obvious solution to her and, in retrospect, showed that she thought about things other than Elvis Presley (it was the late 1950s), it irritated dad. He dismissed her comment out of hand.

Dad had no knowledge of economics; his view was simply based on common sense. He knew that real wealth had nothing to do with pieces of paper or even of gold coins. But if my sister was indeed seriously misguided on this matter, then so are many contemporary economic commentators and politicians who seem not to understand how real wealth and prosperity are created. Money illusion (the belief that money is real wealth and not simply a token) was not confined only to my sister's mind so many years ago; it is alive, well and widespread now.

Illusions and delusions of all kinds can hide out in today's complex world. So much padding makes the truth hard to dig out. It is a happy hunting ground for charlatans, so-called experts, those with an agenda, fools and the incompetent. At times the truth can be dug out, and the meretricious unmasked, by going to a ruder state of society; by peeling away the padding. Of course, this won't always work and can get stretched and tedious if taken too far. But, used sparingly, it is useful for separating fact from fancy. Economics, properly understood and defined, is a powerful tool for revealing the truth once the padding is gone. This is the case, for example, in considering the economics of income redistribution and the entitlement agenda pursued by governments, various welfare lobbies, and sections of the media.

My grandmother and sister knew nothing about economics.

Their views were wrong-headed. At the same time, they were both unknowingly grappling with areas of economics which go to the heart of what is wrong with the practice of economics by governments today, and why it is predominantly a credo of despair and impoverishment.

Dad's political leaning was born of the class system in England and a view that workers had to stick together to avoid being exploited. This was understandable in the times in which he worked – the 1920s to the 1960s. He gave no sign that he thought he was entitled to things he didn't work for. This would not have entered his head. He was influenced by working men struggling for better conditions. Leaving aside the justice and merits of individual cases, and the simplistic battlelines, the struggles were honourable.

He had no truck with people who wanted something for nothing – layabouts, main chancers and spivs – as he variously called them. Self-reliance, working hard in return for a decent wage, was an indelible part of his thinking. This way of thinking, as straightforward as it is, underscores the role of economics as a guide to hope and prosperity. It became lost to me for a decade or more of my adult life and through a considerable part of my study of economics. Effectively, I became tribally affiliated with those on the left (sometimes collectively referred to as "the Left").

The Left encompass modern-day socialists and liberal progressives – in politics, in trade union leadership, in the media, in education, in the legal profession, in Hollywood, and so on. They believe that free market capitalism produces crises and leads to excesses and injustices which need correction by big government. They tend to see fault in the history of Western societies. Somewhere on the other side of the political spectrum are conservatives. Conservatives occupy a broad church. However, generally speaking, they are those who believe in the primacy of free market capitalism in governing economic affairs and in limiting the role of government. They tend to be protective of their nation's institutions and historical achievements.

Economics has nothing to do with tribalism or political affiliations. It is, or should be, an objective discipline. Yet my own tribal affiliation to the left coloured and distorted my economic thinking for a number of years. It meant that I was not an economist, even when teaching the subject.

Most people have not studied economics. This is fortunate because it is better to be at the crossroads than to have travelled too far the wrong way. The essential elements of economics are fairly easy to understand. The benefits of having this level of understanding are considerable. Knowing about economics means that economic mythologies have less room to lurk and flourish. It means that there is less likelihood of economic despair built on delusionary foundations and more likelihood of economic hope built on realistic foundations.

Economics

Joan Robinson, a well-known Cambridge economist in her day, when asked to define economics, quipped that economics is what economists do. Professor Robinson was a disciple of Keynes and very much on the left of the political spectrum. Maybe relativism appealed to her. I don't know. In any event, she was wrong. Economics is not any old thing done by people calling themselves economists. Economics is not the handmaiden of whatever political philosophy someone may hold. Economics is economics. It stands on its own feet. It is objective. It cannot be moulded to suit whatever political or philosophical wind is blowing. So, to turn Robinson's quip around, doing economics is what economists should be about and they shouldn't be about doing anything else; unless it is in their spare time.

What is economics? There are numbers of definitions. Economics might be defined by way of pointing to the material in standard university texts. This would be unwieldy and misleading because of the influence of Keynesian economics on those texts. Alfred Marshall, an authority among economists in the last years of the 19th and first part of the 20th century, famously defined economics as "the study of mankind in the ordinary business of life". This is a little too vague for my purpose. A longer-winded definition was provided by the Nobel Prize winning American economist Paul Samuelson. In my 1970 edition of his *Economics: An Introductory Analysis* (the largest selling introductory economics text of all time) he defines economics in this way:

> Economics is the study of how men in society choose, with or without the use of money, to employ scarce productive resources, which could have alternative uses, to produce various commodities over time and distribute them for consumption, now and in the future, among various people and groups in society.

This is fine so far as it goes. It covers the allocation of scarce resources among competing ends and the distribution of the goods produced out of this process. The problem with the definition, in my view, is that it doesn't explicitly mention the role of free markets in guiding economic choices. It would fit any arbitrary or despotic system of determining economic outcomes and therefore could lead economic inquiry down false trails. It also gives no sense of the dynamic nature of economic affairs. It is better, I think, and will do well enough at the start, to define economics as a body of thought that explores and explains:

- How the guiding role of prices operating in free markets produces better economic outcomes than could be produced in any other way.
- How the efforts, savings, inventions, entrepreneurship and investments of individuals and businesses underpin and drive economic progress and prosperity.

This I think captures the essence of (free market) economics, which will become clearer as we go along.

Academic economics at a detailed, and often mathematical, level can be complex and complicated. Academic economists have difficulty in understanding each other. Luckily the essential building blocks of economics are not hard to understand. There is less mystery to be uncovered than economists and politicians would like there to be. After all, there is no advantage for economists or politicians in having everyone understanding and potentially challenging what they are saying and doing. Harold Wilson found this out.

The value of the Pound Sterling was under downward pressure against other world currencies in the 1960s. The British prime minister (and graduate economist) Harold Wilson took the decision to devalue the Pound, while explaining in his down to earth Yorkshire accent to the British people, probably with his pipe in hand, that a Pound was still worth a Pound "in your pocket or purse". Well of course it wasn't. He thought he would get away with it. He didn't. He was rightly ridiculed. Clearly, he would have preferred economics to be more opaque than it is.

Economics is accessible to anyone of common sense. The key to understanding economics is to understand the role of market prices and the role of saving and investing. When these are understood, all else of importance falls into place.

Armed with a modest knowledge of economics it is comparatively easy:

- To form an objective and educated view of economic issues.

- To see through the fallacious and misleading arguments too often used by politicians and many, so-called, economists.

- To separate economic substance from subterfuge; reality from delusion and, no less than, what is true from what is false.

Economics permeates almost every area of an individual's and a nation's life. It is too important to allow error to go unchallenged. Individual prosperity and national well-being are at stake.

Conclusion

Common sense allied with a rudimentary appreciation of economics has the firepower to clear away the debris and find the truth. However, there is lots of debris to clear away, determinedly put in place by those with much less interest in the truth than in pursuing an agenda. In clearing the debris, the focus will mainly be on big picture economics – saving and investment, booms and recessions, prosperity and poverty, government spending and borrowing. At the same time, in looking at the big picture, it is important to remember the small – the economic activities of individuals, households and businesses. The big picture is a composite of the small, not some disembodied abstraction. That is why the role of market prices, considered in the next chapter, is so important in understanding the way an economy works and how it can be subverted by government intervention.

14

2

Prices and Prosperity

[P]rice is not determined by the conscious will of anybody ... if one way of achieving our ends proves too expensive for us, we are free to try other ways.

F.A. Hayek (*The Road to Serfdom*)

Prices are at the heart of economics: prices of materials and labour, goods and services, present and forward prices, actual and expected prices. The price of something is not its value. Oscar Wilde cuttingly distinguished between the two by having Lord Darlington (*Lady Windermere's Fan*) say of a cynic that, "he knew the price of everything but the value of nothing". Value is the benefit we get from having something. Value is subjective and can vary for the same thing from person to person. That Christmas present bought by your aunt, buried away in a cupboard, may have zero value to you. It still cost whatever was its price in the shop.

Prices

Price is what has to be paid to get something. Price settles at the point where the supply of something, from those wanting to sell it, equals the demand for it, from those wanting to buy it. Price emerges out of a complex mishmash of sale and purchase decisions. Price is objective, cold and impersonal. Those on the left tend not to like it. It is not warm and fuzzy enough. After all, if you have only a dollar in your pocket and it's cold and damp and a cup of coffee costs two dollars you are out of luck and out of coffee. That's not fair! Surely you deserve that coffee.

An exchange in the western movie *Unforgiven* has some oblique relevance. 'Little Bill' Daggett (Gene Hackman), the sheriff of Big Whisky, wounded, defenceless, and facing death at the hands of recidivist gunslinger William Munny (Clint Eastwood) says, "I don't deserve this". Munny insouciantly replies, "deserve's got nothing to do with it", before pulling the trigger.

Once the talk is about some people deserving things, it is remote from the unforgiving world of gunslingers and also from economics. It is applicable to a quite different world where subjectivity reigns. Individuals can choose to be part of both worlds but not at the same time. Trying to occupy both worlds at the same time is contradictory, conflicting and contorting. A contradiction in terms is the outcome or, in other words, a "socialist economist". Price belongs to the economics world where "deserve" has no application and no meaning.

Prices have two main roles. One is to ration demand. The other is to allocate resources.

Rationing

When the price of any product (raw material, manufactured good or service) rises, businesses and people tend to buy less of it because it is more expensive. If more of a product is demanded than is available, its price rises to reduce the demand to match the available supply. Demand is rationed.

Does the process work? Well it does to a significant extent but not perfectly. It would only work perfectly if buyers and sellers had complete information about the overall demand for the product in question and its overall availability; and if the geographical pattern of demand were the same as the geographical pattern of the available supply. An open auction process gets close to that result but in the normal course products are not bought and sold by open auction. Nevertheless, the process works well enough most of the time.

Supply and demand are brought into equality by price movements and markets are cleared. Noticeable gluts or shortages of particular goods or services are uncommon. This is because sellers of goods and services are informed by past demand. They then try to match the availability of supply with the pattern of demand they expect to occur based on previous experience. When there are many sellers and buyers of millions of different goods and services, the process of matching supply and demand with a high degree of synchronicity is a logistical triumph of wondrous proportions. It happens because sellers are each driven by self interest to satisfy buyers.

No computer driven plan would ever be large enough or clever enough to contain and constantly update all of the economic and psychological information required each day to match supply and demand for millions of different products. Free markets do precisely that to a good approximation, without any central coordination. In fact, central coordination of prices inevitably results in shortages of goods people want and gluts of those that they don't.

How about the vexed matter of deserving and fairness? It is worth coming back to because it is a question that goes to the heart of the economics. Rationing a product by price brings its supply and demand into balance. At the same time, this balance means that only those able to afford a particular product can buy it. Fair or not, those unable to pay the price must do without. A supermarket example is useful.

Supermarkets often mark down the prices of selected products, as teasers, to draw people in. The shelves usually empty quickly because the price is set too low. Some people who would have been prepared to pay the going price miss out entirely. At the same time, others buy a product that they would have been unprepared to buy at the normal price. It's first come first serve rationing. This kind of thing is annoying if you don't get up early enough, but it doesn't do too much damage because it is limited in its scope. Imagine if the supermarket decided to sell lots of products at lower prices only to those who deserved them. Who is going to decide who deserves them and on what basis? Chaos and all kinds of nepotism, cronyism and corruption would result. In other words, it would be an experiment in socialism.

Market prices reflect economic reality. Meddling, in order to be fair, produces a host of unpredictable and unintended consequences. As ruthless as it is, rationing by price has a transparency and honesty about it that other means of rationing do not have. A compassionate society provides protection, emergency services and an affordable minimum level of care and support to all its citizens. Beyond that, it is best to let price and the ability to pay decide who buys this or that good or service. Society can best help its poorer members by providing them with income support rather than doling out goods and services based on dubious non-price criteria.

Bear in mind that rationing of products by price does not necessarily optimise welfare. There may be a distribution of a good or service which is 'better' than that resulting from price rationing. In other words, there may be a distribution which results in a larger gain in overall welfare. Simply put, a person who can't afford the good or service might gain more from having it than the person who can afford it and buys it. The problem is not knowing and never knowing what this better distribution is. There is too much room for subjectivity and corruption to thrive in any process devised to decide on this better distribution. And that is not the end of the problem of rationing other than by price. Rationing by price allows the second, and equally important, role of prices to operate. That second role is to allocate resources.

Allocating Resources

When the price of a particular product rises or is expected to rise, suppliers of the product have an incentive to order or produce more of it. In turn, this results in more resources (labour and capital equipment) being applied to its production. It works the same way the other way around. If its price falls, less of the product is produced.

As simple as it is, this role of prices is fundamental to the growth and development of an economy; to its preservation of scarce resources; and to its efficiency in producing the goods and services of most value to those in the economy.

A particular resource may be being used to make particular "gadgets" whose price is falling as demand drops off. Demand for an alternative gadget is growing because it does a better job. The business making the better gadget is able to pay a higher price for the resource than is the business making the inferior gadget, and attracts the resource away. We end up with better gadgets. Progressively we get better and better gadgets, and new and innovative products of all kinds, as prices encapsulate changing and developing wants and needs and transmit those wants and needs to the market and to producers.

Prices in a market economy continually adjust so that an economy is producing products which people want to buy and which producers find profitable to produce; and this without intervention by any wise authority.

Nothing is produced unless the revenue from selling it exceeds the cost of producing it. Or, at least, that is the way it works most of the time. Producers quickly discover the flaw in producing things for a dollar and selling them for 90 cents. The market is a hard taskmaster.

The price of a product moves to that level where it is just worthwhile for some buyers to still buy the product and gain benefit and to where it is just worthwhile for some producers to supply the product. There is no better way to do things. There is no giant computer that could do it better. All else introduces inefficiencies and arbitrariness that easily morphs into impoverishment and corruption.

Understanding the role of prices and their central role in economic life provides a sharp theoretical framework to assess political proposals which, to one extent or other, involve regulating (manipulating or controlling) prices. Usually this is presented as being for the public "good". Assuredly and inevitably it contributes to the public "bad".

Everything useful that economics can say brings in prices in one way or another. Bad economic policy usually subverts the role of prices in one way or another.

Prosperity

Today's prosperity in Western societies has depended critically on allowing prices to do their job. New and innovative products are produced because those producing them believe that they can charge a price in excess (often well in excess initially) of the costs of production and sell lots of them. If they are wrong little more is heard about it. If they are right their product tends to crowd out existing competing products whose price tends to decline as the demand for them falls. There are many prominent examples. To name just a few: gas filaments to light bulbs, horse carriages to motor cars, airships to jumbo jets, typewriters to desk top computers, bulky TVs to flat screens. And there are millions of subtle examples. New products are also continuously introduced where there are no closely competing existing products, like the mobile (cell) phone. In all cases, it is price which guides and determines the pattern of production best meeting the needs of businesses and individuals within an economy.

The ability of government to provide and subsidise particular services depends upon the wealth creation of markets guided by prices. The more governments encroach into areas which can be best served by allowing the market to work, the poorer the outcome. Governments operate by fiat. They don't have prices to guide them. They don't face the discipline of the market. Markets provide feedback that can make or break businesses. An informed trial and error process consistently reshapes the landscape of production and demand. It is one of the important reasons why market economies are prosperous and why communist Eastern Europe became relatively impoverished.

Prosperity allows indulgences that poverty limits or prevents. This extends from supporting those who cannot provide for themselves to exploring outer space. It allows the construction and maintenance of vital infrastructure. It allows the development of the arts; the building of majestic art galleries and opera theatres. The import is clear. Without prosperity life can get pretty mean and dreary. Prosperity is a key word. It is best not to lose sight of it. Allowing market prices to do their job brings prosperity. Without prosperity little can be done beyond subsisting. It is vital to allow prices to do their job.

Conclusion

It is possible to say conclusively that an economy within which market prices move freely and responsively to the ever changing pattern of demand and production will be more prosperous than one in which price movements are subverted or controlled by government. Price movements fill in part of the prosperity jigsaw. The other part is filled by the role of private saving in freeing resources for investing in future production.

Delaying gratification is often the key to individual success. Equally a society which delays gratification by saving becomes much more prosperous than one that spends or consumes all that it earns. The next chapter looks at the process of saving and its counterpart investing in generating prosperity. It begins in a coastal village at a time when things were less complex than now.

3

Saving and Investing

[I]ndustry is limited by capital ... capital is the result of saving ...

John Stuart Mill (*Principles Of Political Economy*)[1]

There is no better way to explain the role and importance of saving than to go back to a ruder state of society in the distant past. In this case, to a coastal village near the mouth of an inland river, where a particularly industrious, skilful and ambitious man, called Jack, lived.

Allegorical Villages

Jack caught more fish than he could eat, while his fellow villagers just barely managed to feed themselves. Without refrigeration his spare fishes spoiled. He had an idea of giving his spare fishes to some of his fellow villagers in return for them forgoing their own fishing and building him a bigger hut. When his bigger hut was built he had an even better idea. In return for his spare fishes, he commissioned the construction of a bigger fishing boat for himself and something he had dreamt up in his spare time, which he called "fishing net".

Now, with his bigger boat and net he had many spare fishes, and had the best idea of all. He employed some villagers to help him catch even more fish and sail upriver to neighbouring villages and towns, where fish were scarcer, to trade his fish for other goods and something called money. That was only the start; that village is now

---

1 J.S. Mill's *Principles* went through numbers of editions from 1848. It was the undisputed authoritative text on economics during the second half of the 19th century.

called "Metropolis".

There was another coastal village, equally endowed, in another place. A man in that village, Nigel, caught more fishes than he could eat and it was decided that he would share his surplus with the other villagers, so that they would have a little more to eat and would not have to work so hard. That village is now called "Village".

Metropolis and Village never quite existed in the way described. But something like them has and does exist.

There are a number of things to notice about the different experiences of the coastal villages. The industrious man (Jack) in the first village was ambitious. His counterpart in the second village (Nigel) was seemingly not. Although, to be fair, we don't know how much Nigel was pressed by his fellow villagers to set his ambition aside. Jack was also innovative; we don't know whether Nigel was innovative. He could have been and this may have showed itself in different circumstances. Jack understood that by investing in a bigger boat and net he would give himself the opportunity to grow his wealth. We don't know whether Nigel had that understanding. He may have done; and this again may have showed itself in different circumstances. Whether it was the character of the villagers in Jack's village or the drive of Jack we don't know. We do know that Jack's villagers were prepared to forgo sharing Jack's surplus fish. On the other hand, Nigel and his villagers decided through some process that they would share the surplus fish. And the rest, as they say, is history.

Brought into an industrial context Jack might be an entrepreneur like Henry Ford or Bill Gates or any CEO or chairman of a leading company or proprietor of a successful middle-sized or small business. Industrious, innovative and ambitious, they all see investing their savings, or the savings of others, in the development of their businesses, as the key to growth and prosperity.

A big question in economics is which comes first: is it saving or investing? Economic policy turns on the answer.

In the coastal village tale, the answer is clear. Saving came first. Jack could not have invested unless he had first saved. There would have been nothing left over to keep people alive. If everything produced had been consumed, there would have been nothing to keep people going while they were building a bigger boat to catch more fish.

Jack was able to have his boat built because the village community within which he lived "allowed" him to retain his savings. In the other village, Nigel's savings were spread around all the villagers and consumed. Therefore no investing took place.

Saving was in the driving seat in Jack's village. At question is whether it is always in the driving seat. Observation doesn't necessarily help, particularly in a complex economy, because the amount of saving and investing are always equal after the event.

Each dollar of income is a measure of production of consumer goods or investment goods. Each dollar is either consumed or saved. What is saved, therefore, must be equal to the production of investment goods provided all of the consumer goods are purchased. If they are not all purchased, then they will become unsold stock, defined as (inventory) investment to make the equality good. If this kind of inventory build up is unwanted, the economy is not in "equilibrium" (where everyone is content to keep doing the same thing). In that case, producers will cut their production of consumer goods until equilibrium is achieved. At this point, not only will saving equal investing but with exactly the right balance of consumer goods and investment goods being produced.²

Driving Seat

If saving and investing are equal by definition, then if one increases so must the other. Which of the two is proactive and which reactive depends on the circumstances. It is time to turn to John Maynard Keynes and his seminal work *The General Theory of Employment, Interest and Money* (*The General Theory*). *The General Theory* was published in 1936 when the Great Depression was still on foot.

Keynes squarely put investing in the driving seat. He was driven to this (so to speak) as a result of his indictment of capitalism on the one hand, and his (implicit) acclamation of it, on the other. Undoubtedly influenced by the Great Depression, he indicted capitalism for producing cyclical downturns (and unemployment) that at times might be severe and long-lasting. He acclaimed capitalism for producing such abundance that demand would soon be sated. Unfortunately, the consequence of this abundance in Keynes' view was that the need for work would fall and widespread unemployment would become an intractable and endemic long-term (secular) problem.

The economy defaults to unemployment in Keynes' world. In such a world putting investing in the driver's seat makes sense. To see this it is necessary to understand that in a monetary economy (as distinct from one based purely on bartering one good for another) banks, by

---

2 When government taxation and spending, and overseas trade, are included, private sector saving in any one country need not equal private sector investing in that country. Private investing can be greater than private saving if government saves by spending less than it taxes (unusual as that is) or if imports exceed exports. Private saving can be greater than private investing, if government dissaves by spending more than it taxes, or if exports exceed imports. However, on a world scale, the total of saving by the private sector and by government taken together will always equal the total of investing. That equality holds, as it must.

making loans, can provide the wherewithal for a business to invest without saving having occurred. If there are unemployed resources, businesses can borrow from banks, employ those resources, and make things to sell. In the course of things being made, income is earned, part of which is saved. Hence investing generates saving. The economic logic of this Keynesian proposition is sound.

Equally it is sound enough to say, as Keynes did, that in circumstances of widespread and substantial unemployment attempts to save more might not generate an increase in actual investing and saving. Attempts to save might depress consumption, lead to the build up of unwanted stocks and, in consequence, depress production, investing and saving. It is true that some offset to this effect may arise as a greater preparedness to save reduces interest rates and thereby stimulates investment. However, on balance, the net result is likely to be less saving and investment, at least in the short term. While Keynes was right about this, its relevance and importance hinge on endemic unemployment being the natural order of things in a capitalist economy. If this is not the case his economics unravels, as indeed it does.

Conclusion

The conclusion falling out of the previous chapter was that an economy which allows market prices to move freely and responsively will be materially more prosperous than one that does not. The conclusion falling out of this chapter is that an economy which has more saving and investing will be materially more prosperous than one with less.

Saving and investing taken together propel an economy onward. They are the engine. Prices determine what, and how much of what, will be produced. They are the steering. There is a fractious and unpredictable braking system, considered further on in Chapter 7 (on economic cycles).

In his imagined stagnating world of endemic unemployment, Keynes always saw the solution in measures to increase investing (or spending). His direction of causation always went from investing to saving. He therefore did not grapple with the "eager-to-grow" world in which saving has to be encouraged to accommodate and to underpin and drive investing.

Keynes put investing in the driving seat, with saving a passenger. Critically also, he largely ignored the role of prices. Was Keynes right or mainly right or was he wrong or hopelessly wrong? The answer to this question is of vital importance for understanding the economy: what makes it tick; why it sometimes booms and sometimes busts; and how best to act to put it right when it busts. The answer also points to Keynes as either being a far-sighted genius, as undoubtedly he thought he was; or being badly mistaken, and even a "crackpot". As I explain, I tend towards the latter view.

4
Keynes and Keynesians

Practical men, who believe themselves exempt from any intellectual influences, are usually the slaves of some defunct economist.

Keynes (*The General Theory*)

Finding the truth, as Socrates suggested, is not a matter of counting heads. If it were we would still believe that the earth was flat; that the Sun was the centre of the universe; that miasma caused infections; that the Piltdown man really was the missing link; that time was invariant, and a host of other generally held "truths" of the past. Keynesian economics or Keynesianism has been the popular truth now for over three-quarters of a century.

Beguiling and Simplistic

Keynesianism is the progeny of *The General Theory*, written by Keynes when the Great Depression was still on foot. Although he died in 1946, Keynes is by no means one of those "defunct economists" whose theories linger on unconsciously in the minds of practical men. His influence over the way governments and international economic organisations (like the IMF and the OECD) view their role in economic affairs is as evident and prominent today as it ever was. Keynes and Keynesianism more or less define government economic policy. It would therefore be nice if it were right. Unfortunately, Keynes was wrong about almost everything of importance.

In fact, as I will show, Keynesian economics is no less than economic quackery. It has led governments into ruinous profligacy. It has created an illusion of power over economic events when none exists. It has given rise to false hopes by creating a pretence of its worth, even while wreaking economic harm.

Most economists (who have studied hard) and seemingly all governments believe in and embrace Keynesian economics. While there have been flirtations with other more recent theories which compete with Keynesian theory and its prescriptions – prominently, monetarism, supply-side theory, and rational expectations – nothing has knocked Keynesianism off its perch.[3] President Richard Nixon said in 1971 that "we are all Keynesians now". The policies of national governments in tilting at the impact of the Global Financial Crisis, by wielding Keynesian stimulus spending, bring the story up to date.

Nothing new has succeeded in supplanting Keynesianism because the alternatives thrown up since Keynes are partial and unintelligible to most people and politicians. Keynesianism is complete and intelligible. It has a beguiling answer to the problem of unemployment. True, it is simplistic. However, this has not proved fatal; so far.

Economies are complicated and complex. Each day millions of decisions to buy and sell different assets, materials, goods and services are matched without the aid of a computer. How does it all hang together and how can it ever be controlled? Saying it can't be controlled does not sit easily with politicians, governments and policy-makers whose *raison d'être* is to be like the captain of the ship.

---

[3] Monetarism owing most to Milton Friedman puts the money supply as the centrepiece in determining price inflation and the level of economic activity in the short run. Supply-side theory owing most to Arthur Laffer suggests that lowering taxation rates might generate more government revenue because of its effect of increasing economic activity. Roughly speaking, the theory of rational expectations, first developed by American economist John Muth, assumes that economic agents use all available information to optimise their positions. Relevantly, it has been used, among other applications, to make the case that government policy designed to increase economic activity will fail because economic agents will anticipate the effect it will have on prices and interest rates and act accordingly.

They want to steer the economy away from shoals and reefs and into favourable and powerful currents. To them Keynes and his Keynesian followers were, and are, a godsend.

Keynesianism fits into a mindset which says that problems can be solved. Keynesianism provides a way to attenuate recessions. Governments can spend their way out of them. When the private sector (individuals and businesses) think it best to pay down debt governments are advised to spend big using taxpayers' current and future earnings. On its face, this seems silly and counterproductive. And it is. But Keynes found a way to make it look sensible, proving that silly can be made to look sensible and fool most economists all of the time.

Keynes cut through all the complexity of the way economies work and explained it all with aggregates. He said that if "aggregate demand" (total spending) in an economy is too low, production will also be too low and unemployment will result. This is true, and unexceptional, purely as an ex post description. Production and spending are two sides of the same coin. What was novel and ultimately damaging was his view that the economy might not restore itself to health once it had fallen into recession (at least for a very long time) and, critically, his approach to fixing it.

Keynes was too pessimistic about the ability of an economy to right itself. He was wrong about that. However, the more important matter is the Keynesian prescription for fixing an economy once it has fallen into recession. That prescription is to increase government (public) spending.

As a matter of record, it is important to say that Keynes himself did not simply advocate increasing public spending to make up for any shortfall in private sector spending. Keynes in *The General Theory* advocated an intrusive and continuous role for government. This forgotten relic of his economics will be explained further on. Contemporary Keynesian economists pay it no heed. Either it is too embarrassing or they have never read *The General Theory*. One or the other.

There is no doubt that public spending will boost production and employment among those businesses which are in receipt of the funds. If the government spends money on, say, constructing and repairing roads, or building new school classrooms, or building bridges, or renovating airport buildings, then architects, engineers, builders and others will be employed. Bricks and concrete and other materials will be made and used. The national accounts will show a boost to government spending and production. If this were the end of the matter, success could be claimed as, in fact, it usually is. It is not the end of the matter.

At question is whether public spending, by interfering with market forces and by choking capital markets with government debt, distorts the economy away from its complex growth path and does more harm than good. Nothing in *The General Theory*, on which the Keynesian model is built, answers that question. It is an empirical question, though it can't be answered empirically. The complexity of economic affairs clouds empiricism. Reliance has to be placed on sound economic logic and on common sense. They prove sufficient, I believe, to show that the Keynesian prescription is simplistic, misconceived and damaging.

Keynesian Methodology

Keynes added up (aggregated) all of the items produced and all of the items demanded. The first was aggregate production (or looked at another way aggregate income). The second was aggregate demand,[4] made up of consumer spending, investment spending and government spending. Aggregate production equals aggregate

---

[4] More correctly aggregate effective demand, demand for which there is purchasing power rather than just pie-in-the-sky demand.

demand just as investing equals saving. By definition, if aggregate demand and production are too low, unemployment will result.

Nothing is amiss in portraying the economy in this aggregate form for pedagogical purposes. Nothing is lost if the complexity underneath is kept in mind when moving from description to prescription. Everything is lost if the complexity underneath is lost sight of. Keynesians lose sight of it.

Complexity is a nuisance. That is the problem with all of the competing economic theories since Keynes. They are complex. They provide no straightforward and appealing prescription. On the other hand, Keynesianism has a complete and straightforward prescription that is in sync with what governments like to do, which is to spend. Governments find it appealing.

Other economic theories since Keynes occupy a place in academic niches and for a time may have influenced this or that government but they don't explain how the economy works. They don't put at the disposal of governments the same ostensible power to orchestrate economic affairs. Keynesianism does that; nothing can compete with it.

Keynes has spawned generations of economists and politicians who think that spending money is one and the same thing as making money. In the movie *The War of the Roses*, Michael Douglas in character says to his wife (played by Kathleen Turner): "It's a lot easier to spend it than it is to make it, honeybun!" Well not according to Keynesian economists, it isn't.

The conclusion that increasing government expenditure will lift aggregate demand, and consequently production and employment, is a non sequitur. That has not held it back. The complex and correct have been no match for the simple and simplistic. Keynesian economists believe in the spurious and curious notion that economies are driven by spending rather than by making. Spending has become the measure of progress. There are two mutually reinforcing factors at work. One is the way economics is taught; the second is the formation of a well-defended "conventional wisdom" around Keynesian economics.

Economics Teaching

For the most part, economic advisers to governments have been taught macroeconomics through the prism of Keynesian economics as though they are one and the same. They come away believing that boosting aggregate demand through government spending is the way to produce growth and prosperity.

The key to this is the very term "macroeconomics" itself. It has a clouded but relatively recent history. The *OED* lists its first use being in 1948 in the journal *Econometrica*. It seems likely however, based on a number of sources, that it was first used by the Norwegian economist Ragnur Frish in 1933. The exact date doesn't matter too much. It was not in common use, nor was its counterpart term, "microeconomics", until the second half of the 20th century. Importantly, the term only came to prominence in a Keynesian context. Keynes did not use the term in *The General Theory*; nevertheless he is its substantive father. Keynesianism and macroeconomics became synonymous, as they still are to an overwhelming extent.

Prior to Keynes, classical economists of the 18th and 19th centuries, from Adam Smith to John Stuart Mill (and neoclassical economists like Alfred Marshall and A.C. Pigou who followed them in the late 19th and the early 20th century) conflated the big picture, the nation and trade, with the small picture, households, workers and firms. They did not create an unbridgeable terminological or any other barrier between the large and the small picture.

After Keynes, first year university economic texts developed a sharp division between microeconomics, where prices in all their variety and complexity were on view, and macroeconomics, where the world became coalesced into aggregates. In this world, macroeconomics becomes disembodied from economic life. It is assumed that the economy will go en masse where policymakers want it to go. The assumption is an illusion.

Conventional Wisdom

Built from university up, Keynesian macroeconomics permeates the profession of economics. A Galbraithian "conventional wisdom" has been established. This allows economists to do untold damage in keeping with the conventional wisdom and feel good and righteous about it.

In *The Affluent Society*, published in 1958, J K Galbraith,[5] wrote:

> [E]conomic and social behaviour are complex and mentally tiring. Therefore we adhere, as though to a raft, to those ideas which represent our understanding ... vested interest in understanding is more preciously guarded than any other treasure. It is why men react, not infrequently with something akin to religious passion, to the defence of what they have so laboriously learned. Familiarity may breed contempt in some areas of human behaviour, but in the field of social ideas it is the touchstone of acceptability. Because familiarity is such an important test of acceptability, the acceptable ideas have great stability. They are highly predicable. It will be convenient to have a name for ideas which are esteemed at any time for their acceptability, and it should be a term that emphasises this predictability. I shall refer to these ideas henceforth as the conventional wisdom.

Galbraith explained that once established conventional wisdoms are tenacious. They resist challenges vigorously and without compunction.

All conventional wisdoms tend to start with a simple truth. In the Keynesian case, it is that aggregate demand and production are descriptively two sides of the same coin. A more complex set of ideas

---

[5] John Kenneth Galbraith, *The Affluent Society*, Hamish Hamilton, 1958. Galbraith was of the left and a committed Keynesian himself. You could say therefore that he was a victim of one of the prevailing conventional wisdoms. But that is by the way.

emerges around that truth that may or may not be right or benign.

Suppose a conventional wisdom is substantially astray from the truth (the way the world really is) and its impact is adverse. Under what circumstances can it be overturned? According to Galbraith the "enemy of conventional wisdom is not ideas but the march of events":

> [A]ccepted ideas become increasingly elaborate. They have a large literature, even a mystique. The defenders are able to say that the challengers of the conventional wisdom have not mastered their intricacies ... The conventional wisdom having been made more or less identical with sound scholarship is virtually impregnable. The sceptic is disqualified ... were he a sound scholar he would remain with the conventional wisdom ...
>
> [T]he conventional wisdom accommodates itself not to the world that it is meant to interpret, but to the audience's view of the world. Since the latter remains comfortable and familiar, while the world moves on, the conventional wisdom is always in danger of obsolescence. This is not immediately fatal. The fatal blow ... comes when the conventional ideas fail signally to deal with some contingency to which obsolescence has made them palpably inapplicable.

If Galbraith is right, undoing Keynesianism presents significant challenges. Whatever the march of events, the practitioners of Keynesianism, particularly governments, are adept at explaining that things would have been worse without their doing what they did. And, as laboratory experiments can't be performed on the economy, it is not possible to prove them wrong empirically. What then is to be done to undo Keynesianism? That is the question.

A first thing to do is to understand Keynes' world and how this coloured his economics. A second is to understand the state of big-picture economics before Keynes (the classical economics world) because therein lies sense undone by Keynesian nonsense. A third is to show the poverty of Keynesian economics in explaining economic cycles and remedying economic recessions. This is all tackled in the next three chapters.

5
Keynesian World

I believe myself to be writing a book on economic theory which will largely revolutionize ... the way the world thinks about economic problems.
(Letter from Keynes to George Bernard Shaw, 1 January 1935)

Keynes was not falsely modest. Moreover, he was right: he said that he would revolutionise the way the world thinks about economics and he did. He fashioned the way economic textbooks have been structured and written, and economics taught, for three-quarters of a century. His theories have dominated the minds of public sector economists and the economic policies of governments since end of the Second World War, if not the late 1930s. If popularity and influence count, the appellation of economic genius seems to fit the bill. He is up there with the economic giants of the past like Adam Smith, John Stuart Mill and Alfred Marshall. However, popularity is one thing, being right quite another. Bloodletting was popular for many ailments in the past. The important issue is not whether Keynes was right about revolutionising economics but whether his revolution was well made.

Revolutionary Genius

Economic cycles did not begin with the Great Depression. Economic cycles had been a regular occurrence for some centuries. Recessions (or more rarely depressions) always eventually gave way to prosperity and booms. Prosperity and booms eventually gave way to recessions (or more rarely depressions). Of course, Keynes knew all of this. At the same time, it is still fair to suggest that he was greatly influenced by the particular period in which he was writing. Would he have written the same book in 1936, if the 1920s boom period had carried on, or at least had not crumbled so badly? Perhaps he would not.

It is also fair to say that his book might have had less impact if it had been published outside of the Great Depression years, when people were not so assiduously looking for answers. That all said, Keynes did not think he was writing a book about depression economics. He believed that he was offering a new understanding of the way economies work, whatever their state; and, in doing that, offering a way to deal with recessions and longer-term endemic unemployment.

Of critical importance to understanding what Keynes was about is to understand the state of play in economics when he was writing. Prior to *The General Theory*, the mainstream "classical" (as it was referred to by Keynes) economic view was that the economy taken as a whole defaulted to full, or close to full, employment level. According to this view, forces would be unleashed that would restore full employment whenever the economy fell into recession. Some or all of the following would happen.

- Wages would tend to fall making labour cheaper to hire.
- The price of capital equipment would tend to fall making investment expenditure by businesses cheaper.
- Interest rates would tend to fall making borrowing to invest cheaper.
- Individual market prices would adjust, one to the other, to bring the production of particular products into line with the demand for them.

Acting together, it was assumed that these economic forces would propel production and employment back to a full employment level.

The process can also be looked at in less mechanistic terms. It works just as well. In the classical economics world, for all practical purposes, demand is insatiable. People can never get enough of goods and services. In this world of "insatiable demand", the production of goods and services creates a corresponding effective demand. What is produced is effectively income to those producing it. And those with income will want to spend it or save it in order to obtain future income. In this world, all saving is invested. In this world, unemployment for any length of time (idleness) is not tenable. It would conflict with the assumption that demand is insatiable.

Classical economists did envisage that sometimes the pattern of production would not correspond with the pattern of demand. This, they accepted, would produce dislocation and unemployment. At the same time, they believed this would only be a temporary state until producers sorted things out. In equilibrium, when the pattern of production corresponded with the pattern of demand, "supply would create its own demand" and there would be no unemployment.

Supply creating its own demand was characterised and popularised as "Say's Law", after the early 19th century French economist Jean-Babtiste Say. Say's Law was badly misinterpreted by Keynes to mean that supply always creates its own matching and corresponding demand, without admitting the possibility of mismatches and hiccups. This is a straw man. Unfortunately Keynes used the straw man to distinguish more sharply his theory from classical theory. He took aim against a foe whose characteristics existed only in his own mind. J.B. Say didn't say what Keynes said he said. That makes all the difference to the way to look at classical economic theory as an alternative to Keynesianism.

The classical world was not the world Keynes visualised. His was a quite different world and the difference forms a central and critical factor in deciding whether Keynes and Keynesianism is right, or whether classical economics is right.

Keynes believed that the developed world was facing a chronic over-capacity of production. He believed that the capital stock was becoming so abundant that investment opportunities would progressively fall. At the same time, he believed that as people became richer they would consume proportionately less of their income. He concluded that if you added up investment and consumption expenditure it would, at some fairly early point, begin to fall short of the amount required to maintain full employment. In other words, Keynes believed that we would soon have the wherewithal to satisfy everyone's needs and wants without requiring everyone to work.

Keynes did not believe in insatiable demand nor, obviously, did he foresee the development of new products to continue to stimulate demand. Nor did he foresee the growth of consumer credit fuelling consumption. Neither, of course, so far as is known, did the classical economists. They didn't have prescience. But, importantly, their theoretical assumptions didn't need the underpinning of prescience about innovation and consumer credit. In their world, insatiable demand was a reliable backdrop to economic affairs. Keynes, on the other hand, did need prescience. Foreseeing the possibility of a continuing stream of new goods and services and of credit cards might have saved him from saying that demand would fail to keep up.

As the foremost economist of his day, Keynes singularly lacked prescience. And, more to the point, this is fatal to his theory. Keynes was badly astray when it came to crystal ball gazing, even taking account of the woeful record of others foolhardy enough to put their predictions into print. Why he thought in the England of the 1930s that soon everybody would have more than enough to fulfil their wants and needs is testimony only to the elitist company he kept. The problem was that his flawed vision of the future coloured his view of the role of government in economic affairs (though you might go through most university courses without knowing this). He was an interventionist, as you might well have been in the 1930s, if you held his views about the future. After all, if the private sector could not maintain full employment then the state had to fill the gap. The demonstrated failure of socialism in Eastern Europe had still to be played out.

Leaving aside Keynes' view on the satiable nature of demand, Keynes more or less agreed with classical economists, and the neoclassical economists who followed them, as to how in theory an economy might restore itself to health once it had fallen into recession. To that extent, his economics was the same as the economics of his contemporary and predecessor fellow economists. However he believed that in the practical world things would not work in accordance with the theory.

The theory depended on interest rates, prices and wages adjusting to restore full employment. Keynes believed that business confidence could fall to such low levels that interest rates might not fall far enough to stimulate sufficient borrowing and investment. He also believed that in some dire economic circumstances it would be difficult for central banks to orchestrate a sufficient fall in interest rates. He believed that in these circumstances, individuals, businesses and institutions would be reluctant to purchase interest bearing financial securities and would keep their money in the bank. He called this a "liquidity trap". It would apply he thought when confidence was so low that people would be unwilling to do anything but keep their assets in the form of money (cash and bank deposits). As a secondary matter he believed that prices and wages, particularly wages, were sticky and therefore might not fall sufficiently, or quickly enough, in response to unemployment.

The sub-prime mortgage crisis in the United States in late 2007 and 2008 (which turned into a Global Financial Crisis) underscored in stark terms what Keynes was talking about. Confidence plummeted; unemployment grew; and interest rates remained stubbornly high on a range of securities, even those that in normal circumstances would be regarded as prime and relatively risk free. On the whole, therefore, the evidence from the first stages of the GFC was consistent with a Keynesian interpretation.

But then again nothing happened in late 2007 and 2008 that was inconsistent with a classical interpretation of events. Time had to be allowed for economic forces to work themselves out, that is all. There had clearly been massive over production of housing in the United States but also in the United Kingdom. It also became clear that production in the vehicle industry in the United States was out of kilter with demand. The pattern of production was wrong. Wrong judgements had been made across a number of areas. Sizeable adjustments were required. The fact that this had consequential affects on confidence and that time was required to sort it out was unexceptional from a classical economics point of view.

Whether Keynes is right or the classical economists are right does not hinge on whether recessions might last for six months, or one year, or longer, if the economy is left to sort itself out. It hinges on whether the economy might become semi-permanently stuck in a recession and, much more critically, on what, if anything, can and should be done about it.

What Keynes was saying, which started to make the difference, was that the economy might be in deep recession and at the same time be in equilibrium (where no-one has incentive to change their behaviour). Or, if not quite in equilibrium, so infirm that its ability to right itself in any reasonable period of time would be severely constrained; and, as he famously said, "in the long run we are all dead". What then completed the picture and finally made the substantive difference was what Keynes proposed should be done.

Theoretical Crackpot

There is a difference between what Keynes principally advocated to ameliorate what he saw as endemic and growing "secular" unemployment and what his disciples extracted from *The General Theory* to remedy "cyclical" unemployment. This latter extraction is Keynesianism. But that was not what Keynes was principally on about.

This is conveniently overlooked by latter-day Keynesians, presumably because it has an embarrassingly "crackpot" look to it.

Keynes proposed in *The General Theory* that private investment should be "socialised". He wrote:

> I conclude that the duty of ordering the current volume of investment cannot be safely left in private hands ... I expect to see the State taking an ever greater responsibility for directly organising investment ... I conceive, therefore, that a somewhat comprehensive socialisation of investment will prove the only means of securing an approximation to full employment.

He advocated a "socially controlled rate of investment" to avoid the damaging ups and downs of "laissez-faire" capitalism and to counter what he pessimistically saw as a growing gap, as society grew wealthier, between required investment to maintain full employment and profitable investment opportunities. His commentary in *The General Theory* on what is now called "fiscal stimulus spending" was more or less en passant. He was also careful to say in commenting on the effect of fiscal stimulus that "we have to assume that there is no offset through decreased investment in other directions". The concept of public expenditure crowding out private investment was therefore acknowledged by Keynes, though his followers pay little heed to that possibility.

Keynes saw a wise central authority intervening in some unspecified way to maintain full employment and prevent wide swings in private investment. How this would all work he didn't tell us. He did claim that it wasn't "state socialism", because the state would not need to own resources just to tell the owners what they must do with them.

Keynes' socialisation of investment, as with his wrong-headed view of the future, is largely lost sight of in the textbooks. Keynesians prefer to avoid any reference at all to Keynes' predictions or to his prescription of socialising investment. This is not surprising. It all smacks of crackpot economics. First, you think we will all have enough to live in clover any time soon, then, oops, this will cause unemployment and we will still have ups and downs to deal with, so we need some sage to control it all but, by the way, this isn't socialism. Not even left-wing academics could build a theory around this nonsense, so a textbook model was developed which abstracts a simplistic, but beguiling, model from *The General Theory* and it's that model which now defines Keynesianism.

Keynesianism

Belabouring the point, Keynesianism shuns, entirely disregards, hides out of sight (take your pick) Keynes' eccentric view about us soon having superabundant capital, as it does his benighted advocacy of socialising investment. Keynesianism concentrates on Keynes' view that economic downturns may be long-lasting and debilitating, and caused by a deficiency of aggregate demand. Keynesianism in the textbooks is quite simply the replacement of any decline in private investment or private consumption expenditure with temporary increases in government expenditure. It can be generalised into the proposition that increases in government expenditure can be used to boost demand and maintain full employment.

Strictly speaking Keynesianism also includes reducing taxes to boost demand. However Keynesians place predominant emphasis on boosting government expenditure. It offers the apparent surety of directly boosting demand, while reducing taxes does not. Politics also comes into it. If taxes are temporarily reduced, having to restore them to their former level is not palatable. Moreover, governments see advantage in spending money as evidence they are doing something directly to save the economy. Reducing taxes does not present as many photo opportunities as "shovel ready" projects here, there and everywhere.

Keynesianism can be explained using a simple equation. Without loss of generality, assume an economy without foreign trade (or, the same thing, one where exports equal imports). In this economy production of all goods and services (Y) equals the aggregate of consumption expenditure (C) plus business investment expenditure (I) plus government expenditure (G).

$Y=C+I+G$

Employment depends on the level of Y. If Y falls, other things equal, employment will fall. If these falls are serious enough we will have a recession. Keynesianism simply says that if Y falls it must be because I and/or C have fallen and this can be made up for by an increase in G. Surely it is more complicated than that? Not really. That is the essence of it; the rest is embroidery.

To reemphasise, the very simplicity of Keynesianism is its strength. Anyone can understand it. Politicians, the man and woman in the street, can embrace Keynesian economics. All they need do is to put aside their common sense. Otherwise this might tell them that spending money is not the same, nor as good, nor as easy, as making money. It might also tell them that they have never solved any personal financial crisis by spending more. But there it is: Keynesian economics apparently trumps common sense.

The next chapter examines the classical or, more generally, the pre-Keynesian rebuttal of Keynesianism. Pre-Keynesian economics has the distinct advantage of being in sync with common sense but the disadvantages of not being as beguilingly simple as Keynesianism, nor of offering the same keys to the universe.

6

Pre-Keynesian World

There are infinite possibilities of error, and more cranks take up unfashionable untruths than unfashionable truths.

Bertrand Russell (*Essays*, 1950)

Keynes determinedly set out to right the rights of the past by ignoring what most classical economists always took into account. The economy is made up of many different demands and supplies all brought into alignment by price movements. Ignore that and you ignore real economics and invent a crank solution which simply adds to the economic problem it is meant to solve.

Classical versus Keynesian Economics

There is no single body of classical thought. As you would expect among economists of whatever ilk, classical economists had different views on different aspects of economics. One economist of the same era as J.B. Say was Thomas Malthus. Malthus is famous for his dire predictions of populations always rising to eat up the available food supply and, as a result, giving economics its epithet of the dismal science. He is often regarded as being on the same page as Keynes in theorising that there could be unemployment caused by under consumption and a general glut of commodities. Some would reverse the order of things and say that Keynes was on the same page as Malthus or, at least, in the same vicinity.[6] However, as Malthus was

---

6 Steven Kates, "The Malthusian Origins of the The General Theory, or How Keynes Came to Write a Book About Say's Law and Effective Demand", *History of Economics Review*, Winter 1994, Vol. 21.

bested in debate by his contemporary David Ricardo, Keynesians have an interest in firmly separating Malthus from Keynes. And, as I have no interest in an epistemological comparison of two wrong theories I will get on with a looking at classical economics through the perceptive eyes of John Stuart Mill. His *Principles of Political Economy*, first published in 1848, went through many editions. It formed the text for teaching economics up until the turn of the century, before Alfred Marshall's *Principles of Economics* took its place – with taking its place and extending being the operative term rather than overturning.

Mill was no slouch. We should be very wary of concluding that he was wrong. Nothing of materiality has changed about economic and commercial life since he was writing. Yet if Keynesian economics is right Mill was badly wrong. He won the debates of his day. His logic prevailed. It was all mistaken, apparently. This is not like Newton's theory of gravity being replaced by Einstein's. Newton in his day did not rail against elements of the general theory of relativity by another name. If Einstein had been rehashing an old theory discarded by Newton, most scientists would likely have looked at it with some scepticism, such was the standing of Newton. They would have carefully and thoroughly investigated where Newton went wrong and why he was so convincing at the time he was writing. Mill's standing was also, and is, very high. It is best therefore to be sceptical of a theory which rehashes as new something he long considered and discarded.

There is a broad similarity of outlook in the classical world among giants of the classical past like David Ricardo, J.B. Say, and John Stuart Mill, when it comes to cyclical downturns in the economy. Mill went to some pains to explain how there could not be a deficiency of demand for all products in the normal course. He explains with faultless logic that production creates an equivalent wherewithal to purchase that same production. Production he said is equivalently income and has its *raison d'être* in satisfying wants. Common observation tells us that our wants are boundless. Ergo there is no basis for supposing that demand would ever fall short of production in any systematic way. The logic is unshakeable as you would expect from someone of Mill's stature and he expressed frustration with those obtuse enough not to see it:

> [M]any persons, including some distinguished political economists, have thought ... that there may be ... a supply of commodities in the aggregate, surpassing demand; and a consequent depressed condition of all classes of producers ... The doctrine appears to me to involve so much inconsistency in its very conception, that I feel considerable difficulty in giving any statement of it which shall be at once clear, and satisfactory to its supporters.

He understood that there could be an oversupply, or if you like an under-demand, for particular products. He covered the possibility of over-production of some commodities and shortages of others; noting, in such cases, that price movements would lead producers to make adjustments to meet the pattern of demand. He also saw the potential seeds of recessions in mismatches between the pattern of production and the pattern of demand. In particular he argued that a "commercial crisis" occurs when there is "sudden recoil" of prices of particular products driven to "extravagantly high" levels by demand outstripping their production. This of course is quite different from the Keynesian argument that recessions are caused by a general deficiency in demand or its obverse a general over-production. Mill dismissed this argument.

> But it is a great error to suppose ... that a commercial crisis is the effect of a general excess of production. It is simply the consequence of an excess of speculative purchases, [a] temporary derangement of markets ...

The remedy, according to Mill, when an economy is in a recession (in a commercial crisis) is a "restoration of confidence". There is a close match between Mill's description of a commercial crisis and the

GFC. In fact, if you read Mill you might wonder what value current writers have added. You will also wonder whether Keynes said anything of substance (as distinct from form) that was both new and right as distinct from being old or wrong. Mill envisaged mismatches between the pattern of demand and production. He envisaged speculative unsustainable increases in particular prices and their eventual crash; and he envisaged this might cause a fall in confidence that would temporally suppress production and therefore demand. There is no need to bring in Keynes or any later author to reinvent this wheel.

As to the "old and wrong", Mill exhibited a degree of impatience with those economists who gave demand the lead role in generating economic activity:

> It is no wonder that political economy advances slowly, when such a question as this remains open at its threshold.

Making rather than buying had primacy in Mill's classical economics' world. To Mill, Keynes would have been on par with other simpleton economists of his time and before who had fallen into the error of putting the cart before the horse; effectively, of not understanding that effort comes before reward. He might have sent the young Keynes into a corner to repent with the following recitation:

> [A] person who buys commodities and consumes them himself, does no good to the labouring classes; and that it is only by what he abstains from consuming, and expends in direct payments to labourers in exchange for labour, that he benefits the labouring classes, or adds anything to the amount of their employment ... [Buying] merely decides in what kind of work some person shall employ them.

Using the terminology of his time, Mill was saying that saving and production generate employment. What is bought simply determines the pattern of production. While Mill was right so many years ago, economics, as I have previously noted, does not often lend itself to empirical proof beyond reasonable doubt. What is required is a dispassionate application of economic logic and common sense in considering the weight of argument. This was good enough for Mill. It is good enough today to see off Keynesian error.

Producing versus Spending

Recessions do happen. No-one disputed this before Keynes, nor since. How long do recessions last? The answer is, not long. Recessions typically last less than one year, though those involving a crisis in banking tend to last longer than this.[7] The Great Depression lasted a long time, particularly in the United States. Perhaps those classical economists, including Say and Mill, who thought that economies would right themselves fairly quickly once they fell into recession, were somewhat optimistic; then again, what is fairly quickly?

In any event, the evidence is adulterated and compromised because governments usually intervene in one way or another. For example, during the Great Depression President Roosevelt set in train measures to keep prices and wages up because he thought this would help. In fact, of course, his efforts went precisely against the needs of a recessed economy. This meddling with market forces was quite apart from his disruptive public works spending, which had begun with his predecessor President Hoover. It is no wonder that the United States economy was last to recover among industrial nations under the maladroit ministrations of the New Deal.[8] But putting misguided government intervention aside, does recovering "fairly quickly" mean 6 or 12 or 18 months? How quickly would an economy have to right itself for Say or Mill to be right? How much time would have to pass before Keynes was right?

In fact, the question of timing is a complete furphy. It really

---

7 C.M. Reinhart & K.S. Rogoff, *This Time is Different*, Princeton University Press, 2009.
8 For a complete account of Roosevelt's New Deal see Amity Shlaes, *The Forgotten Man*, HarperCollins, 2007.

doesn't matter. What matters in choosing between Keynesian and classical economics is whether something productive can be done about recessions and, if so, what. If nothing can be done it really doesn't matter how long recessions last; they have to be waited out. If something productive can be done it should be done because recessions have unfortunate consequences for many people, however long they last.

Perhaps this can be said without fear of disagreement. No matter how long a recession lasts left untreated, it would be worthwhile attenuating its severity and length if this could be done cost-effectively and without generating materially adverse side effects.

Keynesians say quite clearly that something specific should be done. That something is to increase government expenditure, which will in turn boost aggregate demand and therefore production and employment. In the Keynesian world, demand initiates a production and an employment response. Are there adverse consequences? Well, if there are, it is not a big part of the Keynesian story. Keynesians never say that anything bad can happen from the government spending more during recessions; certainly nothing of materiality. It is largely presented as an unmitigated good.

Before Keynes the emphasis was on production fuelling demand not the other way around. Say's law says that supply (production) generates demand. In the coastal village in which Jack lived (Chapter 3), the emphasis was on Jack going out and catching more fish. Jack produced additional fish. Once he produced this fish he was able to demand other things in exchange. Production came first. Without production his demand for other things would have been ineffective. But, on the other hand, there was demand out there for Jack's fish, otherwise why would he bother to catch it. Which emphasis is right: Mills' and Say's: production creating demand; or Keynes': demand creating production?

The answer can be pinned down by moving from the coastal village to a sparsely populated desert island. If someone on this island wants some fish from a fellow islander he might climb a tree and obtain coconuts to exchange. This might work. It won't if the fish-rich islander does not want coconuts. What he wants has to be discovered before producing something to exchange. It is not the demand decision that is critical to the exchange but the production decision. It is making the right production decision that makes demand effective.

Demand is a wish list unless backed by well-directed production. Production and demand are two sides of the same coin in a descriptive sense. Both will be seen to move up and down together. Keynes saw this, as did those simpleton economists of the 19th century criticised by Mill, and drew the wrong conclusion. He thought you could operate on the demand side. That is simply not so. It is not the way economies operate. Production has primacy. Well-directed production creates effective demand. Nothing else can. Ill-directed production is worse than no production. It wastes effort and resources. Collecting coconuts that nobody wants is not a good use of time and energy.

If the economy is recessed we can talk sensibly and equivalently in describing the situation as production being too low or demand being too low. The real problem is how to get them back up once they have fallen. As the coconut example shows, the way to get them back up is through well-directed production. Think of it another way. The economy is distressed because too many cars are being produced and too few computers. What is the remedy of choice? Is it to try to persuade people to buy more cars and fewer computers or to adjust production to match the pattern of demand? Clearly the adjustment has to occur on the production side. Mill, and other perceptive classical economists like Say and Ricardo, had no difficulty in seeing this. Keynesians have insuperable difficulty. They can't afford to see it. Their house of cards would topple.

Keynesians faced with a distressed economy don't need to look to the cause. They have a generic remedy. They apply spending. In the example of the distressed economy above, that spending may well flow into the demand for cars, further boosting unsustainable production. Demand is all that counts to Keynesians and any old demand will do.

Nobel Prize winner and Keynesian economist Paul Krugman was interviewed on US *National Public Radio* in October 2010 when unemployment in the United States was stuck near to 10 per cent.[9] He was asked what should be done. He said that the US government should implement another huge dose of fiscal stimulus of at least the size of the previous one ($800 billion). Robert Reich, professor of public policy at the University of California, secretary of labor under President Clinton and named by *Time* magazine as one of the most successful cabinet secretaries of all time, was asked on *CNN* in August 2011 about the faltering state of the US economy. Too little aggregate demand was his diagnosis; more stimulus his remedy. His fellow interviewee Stephen Moore, economist for *The Wall Street Journal*, said that this had been tried without success. This never stumps the conviction Keynesian. He provided the standard retort that not enough was done and that things would have been worse if nothing had been done. Moore was either not confident enough or, more probably, too weary to challenge this tautological fortress. Quackery had the last word.

Krugman was asked what the additional stimulus spending he advocated should be on. He said that it was more important that it gets spent than what it gets spent on. I have no doubt that all Keynesians, including Professor Reich, would have been nodding in assent.

Let us take Krugman at his word. Presumably it would have been okay for the Dutch government of the time to spend money on growing tulips in 1637 or for the United States government to spend money on building more new private housing in 2008? Of course it wouldn't. No-one would advocate such policies. They would be

---

9 Interviewed by Guy Raz on the *NPR* program *All things considered*.

adding to the oversupply of a commodity whose oversupply was at the core of the crisis. How daft can you get? Pretty daft seems to be the answer.

Evidently it does matter what stimulus money is spent on after all. Krugman and his fellow Keynesians are wrong about that. That alone exposes deep cracks in their theoretical edifice. More broadly, their error stems from treating demand as though it were one rather than many and had a life of its own rather than being a derivative of production.

Keynesian Error

Keynesians say that government expenditure is needed to boost aggregate demand and production will respond. The acceptance of this proposition by most economists and governments is why "we are all Keynesian now", as President Richard Nixon put it.

Keynesianism is seemingly logical enough. $Y=C+I+G$, therefore increase G and you increase Y. But as previously noted this apparently logical statement is a non sequitur. It does not encompass what might happen to C and I, if G is increased. It is also extremely static in its orientation. It assumes Y will jump today but pays no heed to what it will do tomorrow and the day after.

Keynesians also assume that any increase in Y is good; like producing unwanted coconuts. Building a bridge to nowhere for example lifts Y in the Keynesian world, as much as making something that people actually want. It is best to leave it to Keynes of *The General Theory* to explain.

> If Treasury were to fill old bottles with bank-notes, bury them at suitable depths ... and leave it to private enterprise ... to dig the notes up again ... there need be no more unemployment and ... the real income of the community, and its capital wealth also, would probably become a good deal greater than it actually is. It would, indeed, be more sensible to build houses and the like; but ... the above would be better than nothing.

A different topographical view of the economy lies at the heart of the difference between Keynesianism and classical economics and at the heart of why simply increasing government expenditure will not work.

Keynes viewed the economy topographically from a height and from height detail becomes blurred. From a height, production and demand are amorphous masses; they are aggregates and detail falls away. This may be a useful way of viewing things for some purposes. Detail sometimes gets in the way of understanding. But detail does not go away simply as a result of it being at a distance.

To recall: the classical economists put a mismatch between things produced and things demanded at the core of the problem. They were micro-economists at heart even if this term was not yet invented. They understood that production and demand were comprised of many different components. This is barely acknowledged in *The General Theory* and in Keynesianism; yet it is surely important.

Production and demand are not conglomerate, homogeneous, amorphous aggregates. When the economy is at full employment equilibrium, it is not simply a case of aggregate production and demand being at a high enough level to employ all available resources. It is more complex than that. It is also a case of the production of each different commodity being matched by an equal effective demand for it. There are many separate commodities and an equal number of separate and corresponding demands. Classical economists looked at the makeup of production as against the pattern of demand in attributing economic stress to mismatches. This micro approach to the economy was lost by *The General Theory* with its emphasis on aggregates.

Keynesianism has a "magic pudding" quality. The more you spend, the more you benefit. What is profligate, irresponsible and damaging in stable economic times becomes virtuous overnight. A range of public spending projects are undertaken which do not pass economic muster. Pork barrelling often determines what is spent on what. Industries and businesses that ought to incur the consequences of poor decision-making are bailed out with public money, usually only delaying their fate or the adjustments they need to make.

The problem with all of this, even if boosting demand ahead of production (putting the cart before the horse) were sensible, is that restoring aggregate demand in any meaningful way means restoring demand to match the productive capacity of the economy. And it is more complicated than that. This is not the productive capacity of the economy when it began moving into recession; it is its productive capacity once it has readjusted following the recession. The world is dynamic. It is not the static world of $Y=C+I+G$.

Recessions, however painful, are useful and necessary to remove inefficient and declining businesses and industries and allow and make room for the efficient and new to thrive. Government expenditure of the kind that always takes place is remote from the pattern of effective demand that will eventually arise as a result of production decisions. Governments have no insight into what this pattern of demand will be. No-one does. And even if they did, they can't simply overlay it across the economy. It has to be driven and sustained by production. None of this should be too difficult to see. It is frustrating that Keynesians, in other words most economists, can't see it. It is testimony to the power of misguided education and an ill-based conventional wisdom in subduing economic logic and common sense.

Keynesian Damage

While those who advocate public expenditure to counter recessions take only a partial and selective view of what Keynes said, he was surely responsible for his followers' grievous error of taking too little account of the complexity of economic affairs in concentrating so much on aggregates.

Keynes allowed the mechanistic interpretation of *The General Theory*, popularised in text books, to go unchallenged. He had plenty of time. John Hicks had set it out as early as 1937[10]. The nuanced Keynes, worried by the inability of the system, beset as he saw it by underconsumption, declining investment opportunities and at the whim of entrepreneurial expectations, to generate stable full employment, and needing direction from a wise central authority, was lost sight of. It is a pity. This Keynes would not have survived scrutiny. The simplistic Keynes has proved to be far more enduring. The simplistic has been cloaked by the simple. Production is equal to demand. Demand is too low. Government expenditure is a component of demand. Therefore, the answer is to increase government expenditure.

The mechanistic textbook interpretation of *The General Theory* seemingly allows demand and production to be manipulated at will at an aggregate level. No heed need be paid to the complex set of microeconomic forces that actually drive economies. And thus comfort is given to those whose predilection is to believe that governments have potential mastery over the ups and downs of economic life.

Imagine that a family member is sick. One doctor says I have nothing specific to help. Keep the patient as comfortable as possible, he or she should recover in time. Another doctor says: Do I have an elixir for you! Which doctor do you choose? When I became chief economist of a bank many years ago, I unwisely started out by saying that no-one could predict the direction of interest rates. This was career limiting. I quickly learnt to predict interest rates and found that no-one minded when I got it wrong, as long as I kept on predicting. I was right about 50 per cent of the time. My reputation grew. Quackery can be more alluring than doing nothing. This is especially the case with governments. Governments want to do something. They don't like to appear to be doing nothing.

---

10 John Hicks, "Mr. Keynes and the classics", *Econometrica*, April 1937.

Unfortunately the elixir of government expenditure to combat recession is not just misdirected and unhelpful it is positively damaging. First, it muddies economic signals. Some businesses survive longer than they should or are fooled into thinking that they can continue without adjustment, making the eventual necessary adjustment more painful. Second, it serves to crowd out the development and growth of efficient and new businesses. It does this as a by-product of willy-nilly increasing demand across the economy and thereby maintaining an inefficient deployment of resources across the economy. It does this also as a by-product of the need to finance budget deficits. Budget deficits are financed by selling government securities and these compete with private sector securities and make it harder and more costly for businesses to obtain the finance they need. Nor does it necessarily stop there. Sometimes governments choose to mop up less in security sales than the amount of their budget deficits. This can lead to an untoward expansion of the money supply and to the possibility of inflation once economic recovery gathers pace.

Conclusion

Government expenditure to stimulate an economy in recession prolongs the necessary adjustment the economy needs to go through and thereby keeps the economy subdued and impaired for longer. Real and financial resources are misdirected. Why isn't there irrefutable evidence of this? First, experiments can't be run with the economy. Second, market economies are resilient and will always at some point recover.

Governments can and usually do claim credit on the basis that things could have been worse without them taking the action that they did. Who could say in those medical days of yore whether the leeches harmed or helped? Certainly, always and everywhere, the Keynesian line is that the patient would have suffered more, if the leeches had not been applied.

The classical economics approach to dealing with recessions is more laid back. Recessions will end once producers adjust to the evolving pattern of demand for their products. That is not to say that the classical approach has nothing to say about speeding and smoothing the path to recovery. The difference is that classical economics works in sync with the complex way economies work. It has no single fix-it spanner in its toolbox and so is not nearly as beguiling to policymakers as Keynesianism.

Keynesianism undermines faith and hope in the efforts of self-reliant people and businesses working as free agents. In its place is the crippling view that nothing works for too long without government. Keynesianism offers false hope. It prolongs recessions, hamstrings recoveries and strings out and complicates convalescences. Like the leeches, it is a quack remedy which holds out the promise of a miracle cure. It is part of a coterie of left-wing policies – confiscatory taxation, government overspending, intervention and regulation – which weakens capitalist economies and makes them more susceptible to severe downturns for which, of course, the quack remedy is prescribed.

To end on a tongue-in-cheek religious note. The message at the Anglican Church service I attended one Sunday was "contentment in frugality". *Proverbs* 30:7-9 and *Matthew* 6:19-33 were the underlying biblical texts. They underscored the message that material wealth and extravagant spending often came at the cost of spiritual wealth. Presumably if spending is as good for the economy as Keynesians think, religious folk might have to leave the hard lifting to atheists?

There is more on the Keynesianism script for dealing with recessions in the next chapter on economic cycles. This is contrasted with a good economics script informed by classical economics.

7
Booming and Busting

It's the economy, Stupid!

Sometimes the economy does well. Sometimes it does badly. In 1992 economies generally were doing badly. When Bill Clinton won the United States presidential election in 1992, against a fairly popular incumbent (George H.W. Bush), it was characterised as "it's the economy, stupid" by Clinton's campaign.

Booms and Busts

Economic cycles are a powerful political as well as economic force. Governments, presidents, and prime ministers like to go to elections when the economy is doing well. That they don't always manage this presumably indicates that they have less power and influence than they give themselves credit for in good economic times. Perhaps if they took this to heart they would be less inclined to think they could resuscitate the economy once it falls into recession. What, in fact, they take to heart is a baseless and false view of the power of Keynesianism.

Many books and articles have been written to try to explain why economies sometimes boom and sometimes bust. It is true but trivial that booms follow busts and vice-versa. How else could it work? It is also true that booms and busts have elements within them that cause the economic cycle to swing the other way at some point. That is the way of things.

Economies fall into recession when the economic brakes cut in. Recall that in Chapter 3 saving and investing were referred to as the economy's engine and the price mechanism as its steering. The "fractious and unpredictable" brakes were left undefined. They were left undefined because they cannot be neatly defined. Economies run out of steam for various reasons. The only thing known for certain is that they will run out of steam. Usually this is precipitated by an economic shock of some kind.

The shock might be a steep and sudden fall in share prices, as in 1929. Such falls destroy wealth and confidence, and inhibit the ability of companies to raise capital. It might be sharp rise in the price of oil, as it was in the early 1970s. Higher oil prices increase production costs across many industries. The shock might be an increase in interest rates precipitated by inflation. Higher interest rates mean that many business investments become unprofitable as their rate of return falls below their borrowing costs. The shock might be the deflation of a specific bubble like the 2001"Tech Wreck". Or it might be a calamitous event like the 9/11 tragedy. Or it might be because of extensive loan defaults, as in the GFC of 2007 and 2008.

Whatever the shock, there is usually more to the cause of a recession than the shock itself. Sometimes the economy shrugs off shocks as it largely did after share prices plunged in October 1987. When the shock leads on to recession it is usually because the values of particular long-life assets have become markedly overstretched. Just as when on tippy-toe you might fall over more easily if pushed.

Becoming overstretched is manifest in untoward price rises and investments in particular classes of assets. This generally occurs when expectations of the future strength and durability of economic buoyancy prove to be unfounded. In retrospect, it becomes clear that investments in one or more classes of assets were overdone. It becomes clear that the prices for such assets rose too steeply to create what is often called a bubble. In the GFC it was the price of houses, particularly in the United States, that had risen far beyond a sustainable level.

Currency debasement is a major cause of asset bubbles. At the least, asset bubbles would have difficulty in gaining strength without currency debasement. Currency debasement occurs when money (cash and bank deposits) grows more quickly than is warranted to keep an economy growing sustainably. It is not possible to be more definitive than that. The science is inexact. Retrospectively it is discovered that the money supply has grown too quickly when untoward price inflation occurs in goods and services and/or in assets.

Currency debasement in past times was caused by rulers short changing the amount of gold or silver in coins. Now, the same effect can be produced by central banks keeping monetary policy too lax. That is, by keeping official interest rates too low and also by buying securities held by the private sector (now referred to as quantitative easing or, colloquially speaking, as printing money). This encourages spending on goods and services and/or investments in assets. Those assets might, for example, be particular shares or real property like commercial buildings. It depends on what class of assets is closely associated with economic buoyancy. It may also depend on manipulation of markets by government (which, as explained in the next chapter, was a complicit factor in the unsustainable buoyancy in the United States' housing market prior to the sub-prime crisis and the subsequent GFC). It may depend on psychological factors which see particular markets driven by irrational exuberance – from Dutch tulip bulbs in the 17th century to the internet driven technology bubble in the lead up to the Tech Wreck of 2001.

Sometimes it is hard to pin down why the market becomes over-exuberant about a particular class of assets and drives their price excessively high. It is in the nature of the market that it suffers from mood swings.

It is important to note that it doesn't really matter if goods and assets with a short shelf-life are driven up in price and therefore over-produced, provided the problem is not systemic. The economy can easily accommodate and adjust for temporary mismatches between supply and demand.

When particular long-life assets are being driven up in price and oversupplied, the economy is unbalanced. The situation is dysfunctional. In a numbers of years leading up to the GFC, banks in the United States were pouring money into housing without economic rationale. Resources were drawn to the assets being oversupplied. The availability of those resources for other purposes was effectively reduced.

In a bubble, investments in assets outside of the favoured asset class are artificially depressed. This is disguised. It is not obvious. No-one can see the more balanced growth economy that would in other circumstances be evident. What is seen is the unbalanced economy. Hidden as it is, there is a more balanced economy waiting, as it were, to get out once the circumstances are right. Helping to get those circumstances right should be the aim of economic policy. Care must be taken because the situation is fraught, fluid, and complex.

In the first instance, the shock, which triggers a recession, can itself further dislocate the pattern of production and demand. For example, interest rate rises or oil price rises are not uniformly felt across the economy. Some businesses are hurt more than others. Some individuals (consumers) are hurt more than others. What this means is that the prevailing pattern of production is thrown further out of kilter with the pattern of demand. In turn, this causes more dislocation which further depresses production and demand and, consequently, employment. It is a time for policy finesse not for heavy-handed intervention. Heavy-handed intervention has every possibility of further dislocating the economy. In fact, it is very difficult to see how it could do otherwise.

The important thing to understand about an economy in recession is what it is trying to do to cure itself. It is important to understand this so that economic policy can be supportive rather than undermining.

In a recession, interest rates tend to fall as borrowing declines. Prices are also trying to do their job. The classical economic price mechanism comes into play to restore economic health, however imperfect the process is. Prices of assets and goods in oversupply tend to fall relative to prices of assets and goods in short supply. Resource prices tend to adjust in accordance with supply and demand. All this is true but it is too static a picture. Economies are dynamic.

Businesses estimate what best to produce based on their analysis of demand for their products in future. Those that see opportunities hire people. Those that don't, downsize, or reassess their business model, or close down. People assess their own position in the light of what businesses are hiring and what businesses are firing. It is a dynamic adjustment process.

The question that governments have to address is not how they can solve the problem single-handedly. They have to assess how they can best assist and facilitate the adjustment process. What governments can do productively in recessionary times is entirely consistent with the insights of J.S. Mill and other classical economists. It is not at all consistent with the insights of Keynes and Keynesians.

Governments should try to facilitate an increase in production and demand but in a way which hands the disposition and quantity of that production and demand to the forward-looking market. As part of this, official interest rates should be cut to protect the position of businesses and individuals that are constrained, at risk, or struggling only because of the straitened times. Inflationary expectations can quickly fall to zero or below when recessions gather pace. As a result, real interest rates (nominal – what you see – interest rates *less* expected price inflation) will rise and worsen the recession and stymie recovery unless nominal rates are brought down substantially and quickly.

Austrian school[11] economists (like Thomas E. Woods Jr. referred to further on) would disagree with this, on the grounds that it is anomalous to ease monetary policy when lax monetary policy is likely to have been complicit in causing the problem. On most things I agree with the Austrian school. Not on this. Account must be taken of the changed circumstances that recessions bring about. During recessions, the demand for liquidity (for money) grows. Easing monetary policy is sensible when considered in that context, provided the easing is gradually pulled back as the economy recovers. Of course, Austrian economists are right in saying that in the normal course monetary policy should be fashioned to prevent untoward increases in the prices of assets and goods.

Austrian economists are also right in saying that the Keynesian script of government spending and budget deficits, and resulting borrowing to fund them, are precisely the opposite of what is required. Austrian and classical economics equally point to the undermining effects of governments engaging in bouts of extravagant expenditure.

I have done enough, I think, to expose the poverty of applying the Keynesian script. But is enough ever enough when measured against the damage it causes? Putting the script in context of an economic cycle is salutatory.

Think of the economy as a giant matrix of matching supplies and demands. Imagine a snapshot taken of the matrix immediately before the recession; when in the recession; and once recovery is complete. They will be three quite different pictures. A moving picture between the recessed and recovered matrix would show businesses

---

11 The Austrian school refers an approach to economics that emphasises the judgements, choices and actions of individuals in explaining and determining good economic outcomes. It has a commonality with classical economics. It was begun with Carl Menger in the latter part of the 18th century, through to such famous economists as Ludwig von Mises, Joseph Schumpeter and F.A. Hayek in the 20th century and to modern day adherents. It mainly attributes severe economic cycles to periods of currency debasement (loose monetary policy) on the part of governments and central banks.

and individuals forming judgements about the future. They would be responding to movements in prices, wages and interest rates; to opportunities closing down and to others opening up; and to their expectations about these market developments. The clearer they see the future the more likely it is that confidence will return, and investment and growth resume.

Now overlay massive and temporary government spending on an adjusting economy. It is bound to distort and muddy market signals, increase uncertainty, and burden rather than assist recovery. This is not some theoretical nicety. Overbuilding of commercial and/or residential property is often part of the mix causing economic recessions. Government spending on construction projects, which generally bulks large in stimulus packages, artificially boosts the demand for builders and building materials. It is quite likely in a recession that the relative costs of these resources will need to fall as part of the adjustment process. Maintaining demand for them is likely to be the opposite of what is required. Someone wanting to expand and remodel his factory will face higher costs in attracting builders to the project, and may even have difficulty in obtaining builders. They are busy down the road working on a relatively wasteful stimulus project. People and resources that would be guided by price and wage movements into productive outlets are held occupied on wasteful stimulus projects.

More generally, the supply and prices of whatever the government spends money on will respond in ways that are inconsistent with the needs of the adjustment process. They must do this. Whatever the government temporarily spends money on will form no part of the array of products produced and bought in the recovered economy. The temporary influx of spending will have gone. It will have distorted market signals and retarded recovery. No-one will know this of course. The economy will have recovered and Keynesians will claim credit for their spending policies. It is a small wonder, is it not, that economies always recovered prior to the invention of Keynesian economics.

The classical remedy for recessions is much less intrusive than is Keynesianism. It works with economies. It recognises that market economies have within them the capacity to adjust and to right themselves. It recognises that the more flexible are prices, including interest rates, the more quickly will economies recover. It recognises that unbalanced economies in the process of adjusting are not helped by governments injecting large dollops of temporary expenditure. Why it was ever thought this absolute and unmitigated nonsense was a good idea is a testimony to Keynes' and his followers' persuasive power rather than to their judgement and the soundness of their economics.

Keynesian Script

The Keynesian script is to boost demand as quickly and diffusely as possible. And any old demand will do if you believe in the Keynesian fiction that spending money is the same as making money. Recall that Paul Krugman made that very point when interviewed on *National Public Radio*. He was doing no more than following the "master".

Keynes said digging holes and filling them up would be better than nothing. He didn't go as far as saying blowing things up would be useful if it employed people making explosives and cleaning up the debris. He might as well have said that. Once you don't care what you make, or whether it is useful, it is a short step to "unmaking" things; provided someone is employed by the government to do it.

Part of the Keynesian script includes that the demand must be spread around to have maximum effect on employment. So-called stimulus packages are sometimes about giving cash hand-outs so that people can spend money they haven't earned, often uselessly on imported goods. Or about giving grants for pet research projects that have trouble getting funding on their merits in normal times. That all makes sense doesn't it? That is exactly what people would want their hard earned taxes spent on. But this is small beer. The only way to splurge and spread large amounts (billions and billions of dollars, pounds, yen, euros, you name it) of taxpayers' money quickly and diffusely is to spend it (wastefully) on large numbers of small scale public construction projects that would not pass muster in normal times.

Where else can large amounts of money be spent quickly and diffusely apart from on small scale production projects? Anything of any worth and substance takes too long to organise.

The money has to be spent quickly so that the governments are not caught short looking silly if the economy recovers of its own accord while wasteful and redundant stimulus spending continues. Governments also need to be able to claim credit for the recovery and to avoid, so far as is possible, any suggestion that their policies are crowding out private sector activity and putting pressure on interest rates. There is no time to put in place systems to properly evaluate and vet construction projects or to insist on transparent competitive quotations.

Temporary in nature and competitively skewed, misdirection and waste are endemic in any Keynesian stimulus package. And, the costs do not end there. Further disruption is caused as resources have to be pulled back from wasteful projects as the economy recovers and, finally, all of that debt created to fund wasteful spending has to be serviced and repaid.

Crowding Out

Keynesian stimulus spending creates government debt. Debt is not necessarily a bad thing, if created as part of building productive assets. Those assets will earn income to repay the debt. Seldom does stimulus spending create productive assets. Funds will usually have been directed by pork barrelling, earmarking, expediency, the need for geographical spread, and will be concentrated on public construction projects needed or not.

One of the mechanisms at work to right the economy, once it falls into recession, is a decline in interest rates. Government borrowing and spending prevents this happening to the extent it otherwise would and therefore impedes private sector recovery. It perforce crowds out private sector activity.

Some economists argue that the global nature of borrowing these days has lessened the crowding out effect. This is not so even for countries relatively small in the scheme of things.

Take Australia as an example of a relatively small country. When appearing before a parliamentary committee in 2009, the governor of Australia's central bank was asked whether government borrowing to fund stimulus spending risked crowding out the private sector.[12] He answered as follows:

> [T]here is some potential for that risk ... The question really is, quantitatively, how big it is. My point is that the thing which is most likely to crowd out Australian businesses and other businesses by pushing up the long-term global interest rate ... is not going to be the Australian government's borrowing, unless it is a lot bigger than it looks like being – it will be the huge run up in public debt in the major countries, which are quantitatively so much larger.

This confused and flawed answer suggests that crowding out will be a problem only for large economies, not for small economies. It is correct to say that government borrowing by small economies will put no material upward pressure on global interest rates. It is quite wrong, and inexcusably so, for a central banker to say that it will have no impact on the interest rates businesses within small economies have to pay.

---

12 Governor Glen Stevens at the Australian Senate Economics Reference Committee on 28 September 2009.

The error lies in ignoring the use made of borrowing and foreign exchange effects. And, it pays no heed to the fact that most small and medium-sized businesses borrow domestically, whether countries are small or large.

The only circumstances within which government borrowing would not crowd out the private sector is if the money borrowed were invested in a balanced range of overseas and domestic financial assets. Governments simply don't do that. What would be the point? They borrow to spend and, usually, without regard to meeting any commercial test. In spending, governments use up domestic resources and therefore contribute to pressure on prices. This tends to push up domestic interest rates.

Higher domestic interest rates impact small and medium sized businesses. Neither do large businesses that borrow globally remain unscathed. While the global interest rates they face may not change, the effect of unproductive government borrowing in lowering the exchange rate (below what it would otherwise have been) will increase their debt servicing costs in domestic currency. So, they too will face higher effective interest rates. There is no such thing as a free lunch. And this is not the end of the damage. Debt needs to be serviced. The only way that governments can do that is to chase their tails by raising taxes or by borrowing more.

In years gone by Western governments predominantly borrowed from their own citizens. That at least had the virtue of keeping the debt inside the country. Taxes imposed on one group were used to redeem debt held by another. Citizens had to be taxed to repay other citizens. It was a zero sum game. Now, as covered in the next chapter, neither the citizens nor governments of Western countries save very much, if anything at all. Most of the saving is being done by China, other Asian nations and the Middle East. Western governments need to go cap in hand to international capital markets.

Stupefacient Spending

Stimulus spending is in fact a misnomer it should be called stupefacient spending. It makes recessions worse by muffling and distorting market signals. It delays required economic adjustments. It crowds out private sector investment activity both logistically and financially.

The myriad of market-determined productions and corresponding demands that add up to aggregate production and demand can't be replaced by public spending on make-work projects. It doesn't work. This isn't obvious because markets generally find ways of surviving government ineptitude. Moreover, evidence, whatever it is, will be tugged and pulled until it fits the Keynesian worldview that fiscal stimulus works. This can be summed up as fiscal stimulus right or wrong. To illustrate this, the economies of the United States and Australia provide an instructive comparative case study in the aftermath of the GFC.

United States and Australia Case Study

I will cover Australia first because it was one of the very few Western (in character) countries that emerged well from the GFC. Australia was in a particularly good position as a major exporter of mining resources going into the GFC. The federal government's net debt position was in the black after a series of budget surpluses. The China-induced resources boom had kept government coffers full despite determined efforts by the notionally conservative Howard Government to expand entitlement programs. Australian banks were in good shape. This was not because Australian bankers were more astute than their overseas counterparts. Australian personal saving was low. Because of this and the resources boom Australia needed to import large amounts of foreign capital. As a result, Australian banks were large net borrowers of overseas funds rather than large holders of overseas "toxic" mortgage-backed assets. Their holdings of Australian mortgage assets were sound. Housing prices in Australia (while high on international scales) had not been fuelled by low interest rates. The central bank, the Reserve Bank of Australia, had kept rates relatively high precisely because of that very fortunate resources boom. This had prevented any untoward rise in housing prices.

In contrast, the position of the United States was parlous. Federal government debt was $9 trillion at the end of 2007. Even though interest rates had been gradually increased to a neutral setting immediately prior to the GFC, the housing market had been artificially stimulated by years of low interest rates following the 2001 Tech Wreck and 9/11. The housing market had also been fuelled at the lower end by government legislation and policy to encourage lending into poorer communities. Banks in the United States and the government sponsored mortgage security companies Fannie Mae and Freddie Mac were large holders of toxic mortgage assets. And, finally, the United States did not have the benefit of externally generated growth, as Australia did with resource demands from China.

Now compare the immediate post GFC political rhetoric in the United States and in Australia. In the United States recovery was much slower than expected. The unemployment rate rose to well exceed the forecast level when stimulus spending was announced. President Obama claimed that the stimulus was necessary to prevent the unemployment rate going above 8 per cent. It quickly went to 10 per cent. Bankruptcies, mortgage loan foreclosures and unemployment kept on rising. In Australia, recovery was much faster than in any other Western country. Unemployment plateaued well below forecast, and the central bank governor talked about the recession being one of the shallowest experienced.

In face of these starkly contrasting outcomes, both President Obama and Australian Prime Minister Kevin Rudd (and later Julia Gillard) claimed credit for their fiscal policies. Both suggested that many jobs had been created or saved. What on earth to make of it, that is the question. If unemployment goes up Keynesian policy has worked. If unemployment goes down Keynesian policy has worked. It is a quite marvellous policy tool.

Governments will claim credit for economic recovery whenever it occurs. The Australian government was able to do so relatively quickly and credit its policies. President Obama may also have his moment in the sun, though it was still not in sight at the end of 2011. Nevertheless, at some point, unless encumbered by thoroughgoing and continuous government ineptitude, capitalist economies recover. Why: because they have vibrant entrepreneurial and business cultures as part of their makeup.

The different profiles of the recession and recovery in the United States and Australia are an irrelevancy from a Keynesian perspective. Experience doesn't matter a jot. The United States' fiscal stimulus has been credited with saving America from something worse; Australia's stimulus for keeping the economy buoyant in the aftermath of the GFC.

It can't be emphasised enough that there is no possible profile of recovery that would undermine the faith that the Unites States and Australian governments express in the effectiveness of their fiscal policies. This faith in the effectiveness of fiscal stimulus is common across all countries, whatever their experience, and whatever the profile of recession and recovery in the wake of stimulus spending. Even if an economy were to slip into a deeper recession post stimulus spending, it would be said that it would have been worse without the stimulus.

Take the historically famous case of the New Deal instituted by President Roosevelt in the United States in 1932. In fact, compared with most other countries, the United States fared relatively badly during the 1930s in spite of New Deal pump-priming (stimulus spending). Unemployment remained very high until well into the Second World War years. Most other economies had substantially recovered by the mid-1930s.

Why the United States economy performed as badly it did is a matter of conjecture. Keynesians would say for example that the upsurge in unemployment between 1937 and 1938 was because Roosevelt took his foot off the pedal and tried to balance the budget. Milton Friedman blamed the doubling of bank reserve requirements in 1936 and early 1937, and the resultant sharp decline in the money stock. Whatever the intricacies of the historical course of events, it is hard to say that the evidence of the Great Depression in the United States supports the potency of fiscal stimulus spending. You would have to say that the evidence seems to point towards New Deal expenditure being damaging rather than supportive of economic recovery. Of course, Keynesians will have none of that. They have a theory that is impervious to logic, to sound economics, and to experience. There is an alternative (good economics) script to deal with economic downturns informed by classical/pre-Keynesian economics.

Good economics script

As I have previously mentioned, a good economics script works in sync with the need of an adjusting economy. It has a number of elements. Most should be put in place as a permanent feature of economic affairs. It is impracticable to import them just as a recession hits.

- Product and labour markets should be as free as possible from government imposed or sanctioned restrictions to allow prices and wages to adjust to changing circumstances.
- New businesses should not be unduly constrained from starting up by red tape and environmental regulations. Recovery after a recession depends, in part, on new businesses developing.
- Budgets should be set to be in structural balance. This means, so far as possible, that budget parameters should be set so that deficits, caused by rising unemployment benefits and falling tax

revenues during economic downturns, are offset by surpluses (invested in a sovereign wealth stabilisation fund) during buoyant economic times.

- Longer-term government debt should be issued only against infrastructure projects whose net worth and economic return is tested by objective cost-benefit analyses.

- Unemployment benefits should be tightly geared to training or to finding new employment. They should not become another form of welfare, which in Europe has produced the misery of growing long-term unemployment.

- Monetary policy should be eased to bring interest rates down during recessions, against a backdrop of having a disciplined approach to monetary policy in normal times to avoid the creation of asset price bubbles.

- No extra spending or adjustments to tax rates should be contemplated unless they are intended to become a permanent feature of the economic landscape. Markets, businesses, need to have as much certainty as possible against which to set their plans. Some people – even some economic conservatives – argue that recessions might provide the opportunity for government to begin well-based major infrastructure projects. This is a mistake. First, such projects are usually geographically contained and therefore won't provide widespread employment. Second, they take a lengthy time to get off the ground and are long-lasting. Recessions will have ended before they have got into their stride. Third, decisions made during recessionary times are less likely to be well-made. Programs of major infrastructure construction should be set well in advance. Again this gives businesses the certainty they need when making their plans.

Nothing in this script says what the size of government should be. There is good argument to say that outside of providing essential services it should be small. Governments tend to waste money because they do not face the discipline of market forces. But, this aside, the free market can flourish and ride out recessions, whatever its relative size, provided government does not put obstacles in its way. It is a matter of having faith in free market capitalism. The more flexible and certain the environment, the more quickly will economies recover. Government can best help by adding to that flexibility and certainty, not by detracting from it.

Conclusion

Economic recessions (however triggered) result from a large number of normally profitable businesses pulling back on their borrowing, investing and producing. They become uncertain and negative about their ability to remain profitable. While economic cycles are a confronting part of the capitalist system, they are indispensible. It must be kept in mind that they serve good purpose amid the distress they cause. Economic progress and prosperity depend on economic cycles replacing the old (and less productive) with the new (and more productive). "Creative destruction", as the 20th century Austrian economist Joseph Schumpeter called it. At the same time, policy should be directed towards providing a supportive, flexible, and certain environment within which markets can adjust, to mitigate the severity and distress of recessions and to facilitate recovery. Pre-Keynesian economics provides a reliable guide. Keynesian economics provides a set of wrong turns.

Leaving aside the welcome backsliding (albeit unacknowledged) that started to occur in 2010 as a result of the evident and abject failure of Keynesian policy — which I cover further on — a preponderance of economists and economic commentators are on record as supporting the use of Keynesian stimulus spending to counter recessions. Public sector economists have patently supported it. Bank and other private sector economists are often quoted as supporting it. And, for the most part, economic commentators and columnists in the media support it. Even that stalwart of fiscal conservatism, the IMF, buckled to its allure at the beginning of 2008 when the GFC was biting.[13] The G20 governments support it. Almost certainly the United Nations General Assembly supports it. If nothing else that should cause pause for thought.

Recessions are not the time to build pyramids, to dig Keynesian holes in the ground and fill them up. What cannot be afforded in good times certainly cannot be afforded in bad. That applies to nations and communities as much as it does to individuals. There is no magic pudding. If resources are applied on unnecessary make-work projects, it makes it harder for businesses to attract and employ those resources for useful real wealth-building purposes.

The next chapter carries on the theme of economic cycles in specifically considering the GFC. There is more on the poverty of Keynesianism and the need to return to pre-Keynesian economic principles to better deal with the inevitable ups and downs of economic affairs.

---

13 The IMF's then managing director Dominique Strauss-Kahn voiced his support for expansionary fiscal policy at the World Economic Forum in Davos in January 2008.

8

Holy Holes in the Economy! The GFC

Getting and spending, we lay waste our powers.
William Wordsworth

As predictable as it might have been in retrospect (with those billions and billions of dollars of shonky, made-in-the-USA, securitised loans finding their way onto bank balance sheets around the world) when catastrophe happens it takes most people by surprise. How else could it happen? If it didn't surprise most people, it wouldn't happen.

Salutary Unpredicted Tale

Federal Reserve chairman Alan Greenspan was intent on keeping monetary policy accommodating. China and India had emerged as new economic power houses. This together with a decade and a half of uninterrupted economic growth prompted speculation that pronounced economic cycles were things of the past. That, of course, was never going to be the case. It is not in the nature of capitalist economies to travel endlessly in the same direction. Downturns and crises have always been, and always will be, part of capitalist economies. That said, the GFC was a gobsmacking crisis. And, befitting such a crisis, there was proportionate overreaction.

The GFC prompted more grandstanding from governments,

financial regulators and international economic agencies, like the IMF, than had been seen for a long time. Governments were needed, or so they thought, in order to save the world.

That is hardly ever a good thing. They had at their disposal Keynesian economics and were not afraid to wield it. And, as a soul mate to Keynesian economics, they contemplated the prospect of more financial regulation to curb the excesses of untrammelled capitalism. They were oblivious to the fact that capitalism had long since been compromised by government regulation and that government legislation and regulation – particularly in the United States – had already misshaped the financial system.

This was an opportunity too for those cowed Keynesian interventionists (and socialists) to come out of the closet. Or, as it were, out of their bat cave replete with their capes and daring-do. "Holy holes in the economy Batman!" The GFC provided a platform for Keynesian economists to strut their stuff with resuscitated vigour.

Caped Crusaders

Enter, as examples, renowned Keynesian scholars Robert Skidelsky and Paul Davidson. Both Skidelsky[14] and Davidson[15] wrote books inspired by the GFC. Both were passionate in their advocacy of Keynesianism.

Skidelsky and Davidson saw particular relevancy in Keynes' emphasis on uncertainty, in understanding the cause of the GFC and in putting in place measures to mute future financial and economic downturns. Not surprisingly they saw more involvement by regulators and government as being the answer.

And there was much more from Keynesian economists. For example, Nobel Prize winner, Paul Krugman, wrote in almost

---

14 Robert Skidelsky, Keynes-*The Return of the Master*, Allen Lane, 2009.
15 Paul Davidson, *The Keynes Solution*, Palgrave Macmillan, 2009.

righteous vindication:

> Once again the crucial question of how to create enough demand to make use of the economy's capacity has become crucial. Depression economics is back ... The answer, almost surely, is good old Keynesian fiscal stimulus ... Maynard Keynes – the economist who made sense of the Great Depression – is now more relevant than ever.[16]

What would unrepentant Keynesians and closet socialists have ever done without the GFC? It must have been frustrating to see capitalist economies flourish for so long; to have a script without the right stage setting.

Turning to Keynes

Keynes in *The General Theory* laid great stress on the role of expectations, based on flimsy evidence of what an uncertain future might look like, in guiding investment decisions. This, he argued, made the system sensitive to news and susceptible to collapse when valuations became overstretched. Keynes was undoubtedly right about that as was J.S. Mill before him in drawing attention to the need for a restoration of confidence to end commercial crises. He was right in laying emphasis on expectations and confidence in explaining why economic fluctuations might at times be acute. And, correspondingly, why falls in interest rates might not be sufficient to cause an immediate rebound in investment once expectations become moribund. However this does not explain why particular crises arise nor does it point to appropriate remedial action.

Capitalist economies are unstable. They do go through periods of boom and busts. Did this account for the GFC? In a sense, of course it did. But it is puerile to think this provides anything but a trivial explanation. It is also clueless and politically opportunistic to think that compromising capitalism with doses of government intervention

---

16 Paul Krugman, *The Return of Depression Economics and the Crisis of 2008*, Penguin, 2008.

is the key to remedying the situation.

Quite apart from the intrinsic flaws in Keynesianism which I have already laid bare, the problem with saying, in 2008, that "economies have turned down so let's turn to Keynes", is that the world immediately preceding the GFC was far removed from the world Keynes saw developing when he was looking ahead in the 1930s.

Soothsayer Keynes

As previously explained, Keynes put investing rather than saving in the driver's seat because he thought capitalist economies defaulted to a state of unemployment. More generally he saw laissez-faire capitalism having two intrinsic characteristics that would lead to unemployment at a cyclical and secular level. To recapitulate: apart from generating booms and distressing busts, he saw capitalism becoming a victim of its own success in creating an abundant capital stock.

Capitalism is guilty of generating booms and busts. But energising and enervating capitalism is also the only system that will ensure prosperity and freedom. Keynes' proposal that it be controlled by socialising investment is hardly ever referred to by Keynesians. As previously noted, this is because it is embarrassingly silly.

The second characteristic, creating an abundant capital stock, would, he predicted, result in endemic unemployment by reducing investment opportunities. It would also make societies richer and, in doing that, lessen the proportion of their income spent on consumption goods. Less investment and less consumption expenditure equals more unemployment. This was the world Keynes saw developing, and relatively quickly.

In predicting that capitalism would produce an abundant capital stock, Keynes entered the precarious and tenuous world of prophesying. Others have gone there. Bill Gates apparently thought that no-one would need more than 640Kb. The famous

American economist Irving Fisher thought that shares had reached a permanently high plateau immediately before the Great Depression. Lord Kelvin apparently thought that manned flight in heavier than air machines was impossible. And so on and so on. Any computer search using a computer with more than 640Kb capacity will reveal many false and, with hindsight, ludicrous and laughable predictions. Some are still being made by the foolhardy. President Obama in his inauguration speech in 2009 said "we will harness the sun and the winds and the soil to fuel our cars and run our factories". Really, you might say. Exactly when will that happen? His get-out was not putting a time to it.

To be clear, the near future is uncertain and the far future unknowable. If anyone is in the business of predicting the far future, it is best to make it far enough ahead – out of a reasonable lifetime – so that it will not bring ridicule when it inevitably proves to be badly astray.

Keynes of *The General Theory* believed in 1936 that abundance was within grasp:

> I should guess that a properly run community ... ought to be able to bring down the marginal efficiency of capital ... to zero within a single generation ... if I am right in supposing it to be comparatively easy to make capital goods so abundant that the marginal efficiency of capital is zero, this may be the most sensible way of gradually getting rid of the objectionable features of capitalism.[17]

This thinking was more poetically expressed in an earlier essay, published in 1930. In "Economic Possibilities for Our Grandchildren", Keynes foresaw a world 100 years into the future whose wants would be easily satisfied by an abundant capital stock:

---

17 The marginal efficiency of capital (a concept developed by the American economist Irving Fisher) is the return business can expect for spending one extra dollar on physical capital (machines, equipment, factories, commercial buildings and the like). When capital is in complete abundance spending an extra dollar brings no return. It is another useless aggregate fitting a stagnating, uninventive, sated world. Mars perhaps?

> [W]e shall endeavour ... to make what work there is still to be done to be widely shared as possible. We shall once more value ends above means and prefer the good to the useful. We shall honour those who can teach us to pluck the hour of the day virtuously and well, the delightful people who are capable of taking direct enjoyment in things, the lilies of the field who toil not, neither do they spin.

Thankfully Keynes is proving to be on a par with most prophets – extremely poor at it. The brave new world he foresaw might have been pleasing to him and his Bloomsbury chums; to most (I suspect) it would be insufferable. But that is a matter of taste and, in any event, is by the way. The substantive point is that "want" and "scarcity" still abound in spite of increasing material wealth. Investment opportunities show no signs of declining. Western societies show no inclination to over-save. In fact, the reverse is the case. Keynes' "fundamental psychological rule of any modern community that, when its real income is increased, it will not increase its consumption by an equal absolute amount, so that a greater absolute amount must be saved" (*The General Theory*), has proved to be not so fundamental after all.

Saving MIA

A steep decline in household savings occurred in most of the industrialised world in the fifteen years leading up to the GFC. OECD figures show that the weighted average saving rate for the eighteen OECD countries, whose figures go back that far, had more than halved between 1992 and 2007 from over 10 per cent to around 4 per cent. Most importantly, the household saving rate in the United States had fallen from 7.3 per cent in 1992 to 1.7 per cent in 2007. Other examples are: Australia 5.1 to 2.1 per cent; United Kingdom 11.7 to 2.2 per cent. Of the eighteen countries surveyed only two, France and

Germany, had a household savings ratio that had not fallen over the period.[18]

Saving was missing in action. Compounding the decline in household saving was a steady diet of budget deficits (in other words, government negative saving or dissaving) across most Western countries. Investment had been maintained only by sucking in savings from China, other Asian economies, and the Middle East.

This isn't the world Keynes foresaw of falling demand. As Western societies have become richer they have consumed proportionately more not less. They have found saving to be grossly deficient in meeting their investment needs. Under-saving has become the problem. It is a bit rich in these circumstances for Skidelsky to trumpet the return of the "master" from the past as the key to understanding the GFC, when the master's vision of the future was so badly astray.

Pumping demand in an era of over-consumption and under-saving might just not be the best remedial measure to take. It is rich too, to advocate Keynesian fiscal stimulus in an industrial world sated by decades of governments spending more than their revenue. The United States and Europe are staggering under bucket loads of government debt. If government spending is a measure of Keynesianism, then effectively, we have had almost unremitting Keynesianism. Government overspending has been part of the problem. Is it likely that larger doses will be part of the cure? Hopelessly obdurate Keynesians still think so. No amount of distress and throwing up on the part of the hapless patient will convince them to hold off administering more medicine.

For classical economists, and the neo-classical economists that followed them in the first part of the 20th century, before macroeconomics was rewritten by Keynes, savings provided the wherewithal for capital investment and economic progress. A shortage

---

18 OECD, *Economic Outlook*, No 86, November 2009.

of saving would mean less investment and therefore less progress and prosperity.

Putting investment rather than saving in the driving seat stemmed from Keynes' pessimism about the ability of capitalist economies to generate sufficient demand to take up full-employment production. Classical economists put saving in the driving seat because of their assumption that demand is insatiable. The data is overwhelmingly on the side of classical economists. Moreover, a persuasive case can be made that a paucity of saving was complicit in causing the GFC, lending weight to a classical interpretation of events rather than a Keynesian one.

Causes of the GFC

Millions of words were written in short order to ferret out the detail of the GFC; and still no Holy Grail. What was (or were) the pivotal cause(s) of the GFC? Was it imprudent bank lending; was it securitisation and derivative trading; was it Greenspan's loose monetary policy; was it global imbalances; was it those fellow travellers, reckless risk-taking and unbridled greed? Was it one of these in particular, or a combination of all of them, or of some of them? As debate can still rage over what caused and prolonged the Great Depression, it seems doubtful there will ever be agreement on what caused the GFC.

One of the more imaginative views from the left is in Graham Turner's *Credit Crunch*.[19] He suggests that the GFC stemmed from corporations boosting their profits at the expense of workers by shifting production offshore with complicit and conspiratorial governments inducing rises in housing prices to keep the workers compliant and preoccupied. Rather, I suppose, like pornography was used in Oceania by the Party (in George Orwell's *1984*) to keep the proles docile and otherwise engaged.

---

19 Graham Turner, *The Credit Crunch*, Pluto Press 2008.

There were Obama fairies at the bottom of the garden in David Korten's *Agenda for a New Economy*.[20] Wall Street, market fundamentalism and free trade were identified as culprits, with an attendant "hope" that President Obama would make a speech promising, among other things, that "we will build our infrastructure around the model of walkable, bicycle-friendly communities", with local and national food and energy (renewable of course) independence while, at the same time, giving "all people ... the opportunity to own their own house ... to assure access by every person to quality health care, education and other essential services ... progressive wage and benefit rules", and so on in the same vein. And, all of this, without Wall Street, market capitalism and free trade. Korten despondently thought his hope would be unfulfilled. We can but desperately hope he is right.

The GFC brought Keynesians and socialists to centre stage with as much sanctimonious moralising about the flaws in capitalism as they could muster. In Australia, it produced a road to Damascus experience by converting an erstwhile economic conservative prime minister (or so he had claimed) into a social democrat. The then Australian Prime Minister Kevin Rudd laid this out in a very long epistle published in a left-leaning Australian magazine.[21] How he found time with all his prime-ministerial stuff to do, who knows.

The GFC did not quite have that life-changing impact on Barack Obama or on a number of European leaders who were all on the left before the GFC. However, it is likely to have further convinced them that they had been right all along. Basically it doesn't matter how much left-wing policies damage the capitalist system, if anything goes wrong it is the fault of capitalism. More doses of government intervention are required. It is like those medically applied leeches of times past; if ten make you worse, it's for the want of twenty.

---

20 David Korten, *Agenda for a New Economy*, BK, 2009.
21 Kevin Rudd, "The Global Financial Crisis, *The Monthly*, February 2009.

Most accounts of the GFC laid much of the blame squarely on capitalist greed and reckless behaviour; some assumed it spelt the end of capitalism as we know it. Ross Garnaut's account[22] was one of the few to avoid these pitfalls in their egregious forms. He provides a fairly comprehensive (and more balanced than most) take on the GFC. While Garnaut pointed to what he called imbalances, "clever money", and greed as being important in understanding the GFC, as did many accounts, he took a step out of the usual porridge of ideas to question "the Bernanke view".

Before becoming chairman of the Federal Reserve, Ben Bernanke gave a lecture entitled, "Global Savings Glut and the United States Current Account Deficit".[23] He claimed that a glut of savings in the Asian world was responsible for the shortage of saving in the Western world, particularly in the United States.

On a world scale saving and investment are by definition equal (Chapter 3). Therefore, if one part of the world saves a lot and invests less, the other part must, correspondingly, save less and invest more. Without getting into the complexity of the argument, Bernanke attributed the shortage of US savings to Asian over-saving. Garnaut qualifies the Bernanke view by effectively saying, hold on, it takes two to tango. He refers the "dearth of savings" in what he calls the "Anglosphere" as independently contributing to global imbalances.

Garnaut's qualification of Bernanke's view is instructive for exploring the role of saving or, more particularly, the shortage of saving in most Western countries (not just the Anglosphere) in contributing to the GFC. A first point to make is that a shortage of saving across most Western countries did not alone cause the GFC. As with many disastrous events, there was a series of contributory factors working together. At the same time, a shortage of saving was

---

22 Ross Garnaut, *The Great Crash of 2008*, MUP, 2009.
23 Sandridge Lecture, 14 April 2005.

an important backdrop to what occurred and, almost certainly, was (and continues to be) a more fundamental fault line than any of the factors commonly suggested as being pivotal in causing the GFC. This can be appreciated by considering those factors under three headings:

- Lending and Derivatives
- Greenspan's Largess
- Greed and Risk-taking.

Lending and Derivatives

Whatever else was underlying or complicit, the GFC stemmed from United States' banks making poor quality (sub-prime) housing loans; and many of them. Though poor quality lending for housing was occurring elsewhere, particularly in the United Kingdom, size matters and the substantive problem originated in the United States.

Housing loans were securitised. Fannie Mae and Freddie Mac were willing purchasers and on-sellers of these securities. Unsurprisingly, given the quality of the assets underlying them, they were worth much less than their face value. They were junk or near junk. Investment banks, and their financial engineers, diced and spliced and created derivative instruments out of them. This obscured their risk and magnified their spread among institutions in the United States and elsewhere. Rating agencies were fooled into giving them inappropriate ratings and, therefore, into giving false comfort.

While securitisation and derivates made the problem systematic and widespread, it is still true to say their effect was of second order. Securitisation and derivatives don't compromise safety, if the underlying assets are safe. Why the underlying assets were unsafe is the important question. And, as in so many cases when markets fail, there is the distorting and offending hand of government.

In this case, the *Community Reinvestment Act* (CRA) was the distorting and offending hand. This *Act* passed by Jimmy Carter in 1977, and subsequently strengthened by Bill Clinton, encouraged poor lending practices by "obliging" United States' banks to provide housing loans to disadvantaged communities. Under Clinton, regulatory approval for bank mergers and acquisitions were made at least partially dependent on meeting quantitative *CRA* performance hurdles – lending into particular neighbourhoods and to disadvantaged segments of the population.

This is "progressive" government interference at its most damaging. On the one hand, you have banks supervised by the Fed to ensure, among other things, that their lending is sound and secure. On the other, you have the Administration and Congress cajoling banks into lending to people who have little chance of repaying the debt; often channelled through left-wing community organisations. At the same time as banks were being prompted to lend to people who couldn't repay their mortgage loans, government-sponsored Freddie and Fannie, as willing buyers of such mortgage assets, effectively made lending practices more cavalier by taking much of the risk off banks' books. Hapless banks meeting Fannie and Freddie was like Bonnie meeting Clyde. And, when it all went wrong, it was apparently the fault of free enterprise capitalism. Go figure that out!

Irresponsible lending was heavily complicit in causing the GFC; that is clear. It is also important to note that for each loan there was a borrower. Maybe, so far as some borrowers were concerned – "the banks made me do it". But banks don't haul borrowers through the door and make them sign loan contracts. Well, anyway, not for the most part.

In fact, banks were scrambling for funds to lend. Where banks used to fund their lending from their own deposits, this was no longer possible. There was an evident and endemic shortage of saving. In fact, securitisation and the creation of exotic derivative instruments can be thought of, at least in part, as "plumage" to attract savings in a

Western world of scarcity.

The counterpart of a shortage of saving is a spending and borrowing culture. It was this, arguably, that was as fundamental to the growth of default-laden loans, as banks were in satisfying the demand for them. Greenspan was also playing his part.

Greenspan's Largess

As Federal Reserve Chairman during the aftermath of the 2001 "Tech Wreck" and then 9/11, Greenspan presided over an extended period of accommodating ('loose') monetary policy designed to keep the United States economy afloat. The fed funds rate[24] was brought down from 6.5 per cent at the end of 2000 to as low as 1.0 per cent in mid 2003 and did not get back to a more "normal" or "neutral" rate of 4.5 to 5.0 per cent until 2006.

Loose monetary policy, as with any currency debasement, tends to increase price inflation of goods and services or of assets (or of both) as money is borrowed and spent or invested.

In this case, goods and services inflation was largely kept in check by low priced imports flowing in from China. The counterpart of this was a worsening United States' trade balance. Other things equal, this loose monetary policy would have been punished by a sharply falling US dollar (and consequently rising interest rates) as the price of attracting overseas capital to offset the trade imbalance. In this case, because of the status of the US dollar as the international reserve currency, China, most importantly, but also Japan, oil exporters, and others, were willing holders of United States' assets. As a result, the value of the US dollar fell only modestly against the Chinese Yuan and

---

24 The federal funds rate is the interest rate at which banks in the US lend balances at the Federal Reserve to other banks overnight. The New York Fed fixes this rate by trading in government securities, selling securities when it wants to mop up available balances and buying them when it wants to increase balances.

other major currencies during the period from 2000 to 2007. There was little or no price to pay for loose monetary policy. Consequently, asset prices in the United States, particularly residential property prices, grew strongly.

The question is what part loose money played in causing the GFC? It played a part. It was an important factor in driving up asset prices and so was responsible, in part, for their eventual fall. After all, assets prices have to rise before they fall; they don't usually fall from a depressed level. However, there is no right level of assets prices. If property prices double they are not bound to fall. They will fall, and precipitously, if a substantial number of those who have borrowed to purchase property are unable to service the debt, usually because of changed circumstances.

In the case of the GFC, large numbers of housing borrowers simply couldn't service the debt, almost from the get-go. The problem could not have existed to nearly the same extent without Greenspan, or for that matter without China. But, with a higher propensity to save, the effect of loose monetary policy would not have been so acute and again, in part, it comes back to a shortage of saving. The preparedness of so many to incur unsustainable debt and (in general) to spend and borrow rather than to save was complicit in the course of events. Why the propensity to save has fallen over recent decades is therefore an important question to answer. Reckless risk-taking and greed may come into to play, though not (I suggest) of the kind of risk-taking and greed talked about in most accounts of the GFC.

Greed and Risk-Taking

When financial affairs have gone badly wrong evidence of greed and untoward risk-taking in pursuit of undue enrichment is bound to be uncovered; particularly among bankers and investment bankers. Perspective is needed in forming conclusions. My own short tale is instructive.

I once took out a margin loan from a bank (the deal was sweetened at the time with a free bottle of very expensive wine) to purchase a number of shares. These shares subsequently increased in value. This was astute investment on my part with just reward. Later in the piece, unwisely, as it turned out, I bought shares in a newish telecommunications company. It was securely backed, I mistakenly thought, by the prodigy of a couple of billionaires. I contemplated the rich rewards that lay ahead. I lost all of my investment. This was risky betting in greedy pursuit of unearned enrichment.

Astuteness and just reward, on the one hand, and reckless risk-taking and greed, on the other, can sometimes be distinguished in sharp relief only through a retrospective prism.

It is morally satisfying to be able to pin responsibility on suspect people doing suspect things. There they were walking around with responsible highly paid jobs in conservative suits and all the time harbouring reckless and greedy thoughts. Judgements are formed when the music has stopped; not when the music is playing and the apparent excesses are mostly par for the course. The qualification, mostly, is required because life always throws up instances of reckless behaviour and greed way beyond the norm. Some of these have been set out in lurid detail in many accounts of the GFC. Some chief executives and their acolytes, among them "fat cat bankers" as Obama once presidentially called them, were paid exorbitantly; even by the standards of boom times. However, perspective is required. Instances of massively large bonuses (though perhaps unsettling, offensive and disreputable) were symptomatic of the times; they played little part in causing the GFC.

Banking is always susceptible to catastrophic economic events. This has little to do with instances of reckless behaviour and greed. Take the example of the American Insurance Group (AIG). AIG effectively got into the territory that banking occupies, and into trouble, by selling credit default swaps (CDS).

For a premium, AIG issued CDS to insure the holders of securities against the "risk" of default by the issuers of the securities. In this case, the "risk" of default is a misnomer. Risk comes with homogeneity and history. Actuaries can then calculate the probability of an event and set an insurance premium. Betting on the value of a security lies within the territory of uncertainty not calculable risk. Insurance regulators should have ensured that AIG stuck to its knitting.

The knitting of banking is dealing with uncertainty. Banks try to counter uncertainty, when making loans, with a strategy of diversification. Interest rates are also set to take account of some number of likely defaults. There is not the same science to it as accommodating risk. And, unfortunately, as Nassim Nicholas Taleb points out in *Fooled by Randomness*[25] diversification doesn't work in the context of widespread market failure.

The susceptibility of banking to serious and widespread economic downturns is innate and unavoidable. If the economic crisis is serious enough, banks will need bailing out, to one extent or another, as experience has proved. Reinhart and Rogoff in *This Time is Different*[26] make the point that "... for the advanced economies during 1800-2008, the picture that emerges is one of serial banking crises". This can be prevented only at the overwhelming cost of severely stunting banking. Without being fatalistic, or of understating the value of sensible provisioning or prudential oversight by diligent boards and regulators, nothing much can be done about it. So all that huffing and puffing by governments and regulators about the need to making banking safe will prove futile.

If individual instances of reckless behaviour and greed played little or no part in causing the GFC, another, and quite different, kind of recklessness and greed may have. It is the kind that is promoted by an

---

25 Nassim Nicholas Taleb, *Fooled by Randomness*, Random House, 2005.
26 C.M. Reinhart & K.S. Rogoff, *This Time is Different*, Princeton University Press, 2009.

entitlement culture, within which everyone agrees to entitle everyone to more (regardless of capacity) and where frugality and saving give way to spending and borrowing.

Entitlement Culture

Garnaut, and other economists, in recognising the shortage of saving, attribute it to wealth effects. Loose monetary policy leads to rises in assets prices; people feel wealthier, so they borrow and spend more. While this makes sense to a degree, it is only part of the story. The decline in saving had been going on for a considerable time prior to the GFC. In the United States, the personal saving rate had been trending down since around the mid-1970s. Loose monetary policy can't account for this because, for most of that time, the fed funds rate was not on an accommodating setting.[27]

It is difficult to be definitive about why the saving rate in the United States, and in other Western countries, trended down. Complex demographic factors potentially come into play. At the same time, it is a persuasive hypothesis that an important factor suppressing the propensity to save has been the significant and continuing growth (and promise) of publicly funded welfare entitlements. When society takes responsibility for each and everyone's welfare, it would be counter-intuitive to think it would have no effect of eventually, and progressively, eroding self-reliance and saving; and, more generally, of promoting an entitlement culture. And it doesn't stop there. Adding to, and compounding, the depressing effect of the welfare state on private saving is public over-spending to support it.

A shortage of saving is another way of saying that demand is pushing up against the ability to produce. It is a classical world of insatiable demand not a Keynesian world of endemic deficiency

---

27 See Suzanne Rizzo, "A Rough Guide to the Neutral Fed Funds Rate", *Economic Snapshots*, June 2004.

of demand. Saving is in the driving seat. Policies that undermine saving and promote spending and unsustainable debt are therefore witless and reckless. Unsustainable debt is always and everywhere the hallmark and harbinger of financial crises.

Conclusion

The starting point for exposing the causes of the GFC was the generation in the United States, over more than a decade, of vast numbers of mortgage loans to people who had little or no chance of being able to repay them. From there it is a question of identifying those factors that caused this to happen. As in most catastrophes, a number of mutually-reinforcing factors can be identified: the *Community Reinvestment Act* cajoling banks into lending into poorer communities; the ability of the banks to sell these loans, and the risk of their default, off their books to the government-sponsored mortgage companies Freddie Mac and Fannie Mae; and the pervasive spending and borrowing culture promoted by years of loose monetary policy and the growing welfare state. The common thread throughout these factors is the offending hand of government. It is imaginative fiction in these circumstances to blame incompetence and greed; or derivative trading; and, most particularly, to blame capitalism. Unfortunately, the policy responses to the GFC were entirely based on the fictional account of its causes, largely premised on a mistaken view that capitalism needed to be saved from itself by big government.

The policy responses to the GFC are taken up in the next chapter.

The GFC wasn't the end of the world as we know it. Reinhart and Rogoff (referred to above) provide a levelling perspective by looking at eight centuries of financial crises since medieval times. It can be almost safely concluded that the GFC, though only matched by the Great Depression in its immediate severity and spread, was part of a continuum of financial crises. At the same time, being too sanguine may not be appropriate. There is a nagging doubt about societies that may have lost (or had taken from them) the incentive and will to save.[28] This may not be a passing fancy or something that can be largely regulated away, like sub-prime mortgage lending.

The GFC was viewed by the Left as the comeuppance of untrammelled neo-liberalism, otherwise called reckless, greedy capitalism; and the solution: liberal doses of Keynesianism and government intervention. The more objective view is that the severity of the GFC was the outcome of the Keynesian and creeping socialist experiment underway since the Second World War. This has been characterised by government over-spending and by a progressive undermining of self-reliance and frugality. What a parlous position can be got into when everyone makes promises to everyone that can't be afforded. The inexorable and uninterrupted expansion of the welfare state in Western societies – without abatement even under Reagan and Thatcher[29] despite their admirable advocacy of self-reliance – is making debtors of us all. Mr Micawber[30] can have the final word.

> Annual income twenty pounds, annual expenditure nineteen pounds nineteen six, result happiness. Annual income twenty pounds, annual expenditure twenty pounds ought and six, result misery.

---

28 The rate of personal saving kicked up following the GFC. This often happens in the aftermath of recessions as caution takes hold. It remains to be seen how long this will last once recovery gathers pace and the memory of the GFC fades.
29 See Paul Pierson, *Dismantling the Welfare State? Reagan, Thatcher, and the Politics of Retrenchment*, Cambridge University Press, 1994; for an account of how Ronald Reagan and Margaret Thatcher largely failed to roll back welfare programs.
30 Charles Dickens, *David Copperfield*, 1849.

9
Holy Holes II: Woeful Policy

The uniform, constant and uninterrupted effort of every man to better his condition, the principle from which public and national, as well as private opulence is originally derived, is frequently powerful enough to maintain the natural progress of things toward improvement ... it frequently restores health and vigour to the constitution, in spite, not only of the disease, but of the absurd prescriptions of the doctor.
　　　　　　　　　　　Adam Smith (*Wealth of Nations*, Book II, Ch. III).

During the immediate aftermath of what started as the sub-prime crisis and morphed into the GFC, many investors became poorer. At the time, President Obama was making numbers of speeches promising to spend buckets of money to save the economy. The message was being lost on the stock market which continued to fall. How could that possibly happen? President Obama and his economic advisers had John Maynard Keynes and his economics on their side. There are two explanations. One is that Wall Street just didn't get it. The other is that Wall Street instinctively spotted a phony economic remedy when it saw one. It would be sensible to bet on Wall Street.

Policy responses to the GFC
Policy responses to the GFC were of three kinds: bailing out banks, financial regulation and stimulus spending.

Bailing out banks
Measures were put in place to bail out banks and other financial institutions in Europe and in the United States that were holding,

or had guaranteed, substantial quantities of Triple-A rated worthless assets. For example, the United States government provided a package of guarantees, liquidity access, and capital to Bank of America (BA). An extended guarantee was provided for particular funds raised to support consumer lending. This was all designed to support financial market stability. It also gave a free kick to BA (and its shareholders) which, armed with guarantees, was able to access funding relatively cheaply for a "failed bank" and on-lend at a profit. Banking becomes an easy business if your funding is guaranteed and you engage in high-interest consumer lending.

There is point in protecting bank depositors. Undoubtedly, as Milton Friedman and Anna Schwartz explain, the Federal Reserve's acquiescence to bank failures and the resulting loss of depositors' money contributed to the intensity and longevity of the Great Depression in the United States.[31] Apart from mitigating economic downturns, there are sound arguments for protecting banks' deposits. People cannot function in a modern society without having them and they represent the nearest port of call to the impractical option of hoarding bundles of cash. At question is the degree to which measures to protect bank depositors should also protect shareholders.

There is no good argument to protect shareholders in a capitalist economic system. It simply sends the wrong signals. Monetary authorities and governments should contemplate recapitalising a bank or otherwise providing guarantees, only if the full benefits of these measures are recovered up to the limit of all shareholder equity. In dire circumstances, that might mean temporarily taking public ownership during the course of finding new private-sector owners. A joint-stock business and its shareholders are separable. Usually a business can and will proceed quite happily with a different set of shareholders.

---

31 Milton Friedman & Anna Jacobson Schwartz, *A Monetary History of the United States*, Princeton University Press, 1963.

Governments have no role in protecting shareholders against loss; nor creditors, with the exception of bank depositors. The only reasonable exception to this, where in fact bank shareholders may have a legitimate claim, is in that ironical situation where banks are in trouble because they are holding government debt. Usually banks are required to hold a portion of their assets in government securities as a bulwark against losses. It is difficult for them to guard against the default of the guardians.

To the maximum extent possible businesses should be allowed to fail. If they are any good as going concerns they will be snapped up by new owners at a bargain price. Shareholders and creditors take their chances under capitalism. The reason that governments protect major businesses from going broke (e.g., major vehicle manufacturers in the United States) is that they have lost confidence and faith in the ability of capitalist economies to adjust and rebound. When you think like that, the GFC becomes another indictment of capitalism which would simply fail without massive intervention by government. And, in fact, the more governments intervene to prop up failed businesses, the less robust capitalism becomes. In a sense, it is a self-fulfilling strategy. Intervention creates expectations of intervention which, in turn, lessen the perceived penalties of failure. Once that happens, calculations which guard against the risk of failure are not undertaken with the same rigour. Capitalism becomes more prone to excesses and therefore failure for which, of course, intervention is prescribed. Moreover, when salvation becomes expected and is "inexplicably" denied, as in the case of Lehman Brothers, an exaggerated sense of doom descends as expectations are dashed.

Financial regulation

The second kind of response to the GFC, premised on the intrinsic frailty of capitalism, was financial regulation. The main thrust of this regulation was the imposition of increased capital requirements on banks. There is simply no point to this at all. Banks should be required to act more prudently than other financial institutions and be subject, accordingly, to rigorous scrutiny by prudential regulators. They should be required to make adequate provisions for bad debts, and for other risks, based on reasonable expectations of the economic outlook. They should be required to distance themselves from the obligations of any non-bank subsidiary. At the same time, governments and bank shareholders should understand that banking is a business fraught with uncertainty.

It is inevitable that banks will lose money when the economy goes into a tailspin. Diversification and taking security over real property, their only robust risk management tools, are inherently and inevitably deficient when most businesses across-the-board suffer downturns and property values plummet. Within practical limits, no amount of capital can cope with this risk. Imposing onerous capital requirements simply hamstrings banks and leads to the growth of riskier institutions. Bank failures are not a slippery slope to economic depressions provided contingency measures are in place to protect all bank deposits. The way to provide for this contingency is to impose a levy on banks commensurate with the insurance cost of protecting bank deposits.[32] This will not disadvantage banks provided the community is convinced that all other avenues for investing savings are subject to the risk of loss with no possibility of government bailout.

Stimulus spending

The third kind of response to save capitalism from itself was of course massive Keynesian stimulus spending. As I have explained at some length, Keynesian economists (read most economists) believe, as do the governments they advise, that capitalism is inherently flawed. They believe that economies periodically lapse into long states of torpor within which insufficient demand is generated to take up the

---

32 It would be important to keep the administration of these insurance arrangements at arm's length from government to avoid the funds being misspent.

production of a fully-employed economy. The answer, therefore, in their minds, is to boost demand. And it is so obvious an answer that those who don't see it are economic skeptics, denying the truth of the conventional wisdom. Nor does the experience of moribund economies and intractable unemployment in Europe and in the United States following stimulus spending convince them. Simply, things would have been worse without it. That is their story and they are sticking to it.

Conclusion

All of the policy responses to the GFC were misguided and woeful. Once you lose faith in capitalism you inevitably put in place remedial measures which are both unnecessary and damaging. Let me stretch a point by using an analogy. You are a poor swimmer (the government). A better swimmer than you (the private sector) is struggling to make shore. Common sense tells you to stay ashore. But that is not a good look so you dive in and impede the better swimmer who almost drowns. Fortunately for you, the Keynesian economist onshore, observing all of this, will make the claim that the better swimmer would have almost certainly drowned had you not dived in. Your heroic reputation for helping will be assured.

The appropriate policy responses to economic downturns, including to the GFC, is to return to good economics; in other words, to an economics script informed by classical/pre-Keynesian economics. Free market capitalist economies have the ability to adjust and right themselves. It is true that past actions by government have impaired that ability but that seems scant reason for continuing the failed policies of the past. We have to start undoing the harm not adding more layers of misconceived undermining policies.

The next chapter looks at the discreditable role of public sector economists in advising indebted governments and in responding to the GFC, and queries whether the miserable march of events following the GFC will undo their faith in Keynesian economics.

10

Holy Holes III: Pestilent Economists

It is now obvious that the stimulus was much too small ...
Paul Krugman ("What Went Wrong?"
New York Times, 9 July, 2010)

Consider profligate governments: those in debt and getting deeper into debt, like those responsible for governing the United Kingdom, the United States, Greece, Italy, Spain, Portugal, France, Ireland, and so on. Presumably, there are professional economists in the background. Over the past ten and twenty years of government overspending, some senior public servants, trained in the rigorous discipline of economics, must surely have been giving consistent and fearless advice that it would all end in tears. It would seem not. Otherwise it seems unlikely that such profligacy could have gone on without mounting objection.

The Economists

Take the massive government spending employed by most countries to combat the GFC. There was no sign that senior public sector economists were urging some modicum of restraint. The reverse appeared to be the case. Look at the examples of the United States and Australia, which were compared and contrasted in Chapter 7. The United States Treasury Secretary, Timothy Geithner, was an enthusiastic advocate of stimulus spending and remained wedded to still more up at least until the middle of 2010, if his comments at the G20 meeting in Toronto at that time were a guide. Australian Treasury head Ken Henry certainly did not urge restraint. We need a stimulus package and we need it now summed up his position.

The damage that public sector economists have done is almost incalculable. They are without doubt a well-meaning pestilent. They should come with a public health warning. The economics profession in government service has been hijacked by interventionist Keynesian economists. Politics is part of this but it is by no means the whole. Some so-called economists are left-wing ideologues. Most, however, are simply victims and dupes of John Maynard Keynes. They parade their credentials as though they had remedies that worked when all they have is quackery.

As explained earlier, Keynesianism produced a pedagogical schism between microeconomics and macroeconomics that has no bearing at all on the way economies work. Textbooks were divided into two parts: microeconomic and macroeconomics. Macroeconomics took on a life of its own. It was and still is a Keynesian world of aggregates, seemingly distinct from the economic forces at work among households, workers and firms. Keynes and his followers invented a new artificial world which, in fact, has no relationship to underlying economic forces. It has no underpinning. It has no legs. Trying to understand how the economy works, and how to put it right, through macroeconomics is like trying to understand how an engine works, and how to fix it, without regard at all to its constituent parts and the dependence and synchronicity between them.

This is why public sector economists and most academic economists and economic commentators floundered along with the economies in receipt of their Keynesian prescriptions in the period following the GFC. What happened, they must have thought. We spent big, borrowed massively to fund the spending, and our economies are still in recession and getting worse. They had, and have, no unified theory of economics to look to for guidance. While physical scientists since Albert Einstein were (and are still) trying to bring unification to theories of the behaviour of the cosmos and sub-atomic particles, economists, following Keynes' lead, tore apart the big and small pictures.

Learning economics since Keynes requires something akin to a split mind. Would be economists must learn all about microeconomics and the complex way market economies work. Then they must put that totally aside and, preferably, out of mind while they learn macroeconomics, which pays not the least heed to the complex way economies work. Do economists come out the other end? The answer is with difficulty and not many.

Paul Krugman writing in the *New York Times* (27 June 2010), immediately after the G20 meeting referred to above, despaired that another depression was in the offing. He lamented that governments were "preaching the need for belt-tightening when the real problem is inadequate spending". Paul Krugman is consistent. He believes in a fiction to the bitter end. What of those economists previously preaching from Keynesian texts who, in the face of unsustainable public debt, were advising governments to tighten their belts? What were they using for a text? The fact is Keynesian economists don't have an alternative text. There is one. It is called pre-Keynesian economics. It can be safely assumed that they know nothing about it. They are flying blind.

A key question is whether the evident failure of Keynesian prescriptions following the GFC will undo, and finally kill off, Keynesianism. It should. However, though there are promising signs, we should make no mistake; Keynesianism will be hard to dislodge. It is a powerful Galbraithian conventional wisdom (Chapter 4). And more than this, it has a defence mechanism (explored in the next chapter) to almost "bullet-proof" it against what Galbraith called "the march of events".

March of Events

A malaise followed the Keynesian response to the GFC. Government spending singularly failed to restore economies to health and left governments wallowing in debt. To use Galbraith's terminology, the march of events showed that Keynesianism is "palpably inapplicable and obsolete". The evidence compellingly points to a repudiation of Keynesianism, a theme I will revisit in the final chapter.

The key to undoing Keynesianism is holding it to account. Keynesians believe that economies are driven by demand. If private sector demand is insufficient they believe that it must be supplemented by government demand to ensure full employment, and that such spending will always have net beneficial economic consequences. To be clear, Keynesianism says that public spending will take up unemployed resources and spur activity, growth and taxation receipts. Now, if stimulus spending works, it works. It should work to galvanise activity whether a government is in debt or whether it is not

Presumably Keynesians believe this. If they don't, it is a mystery what they do believe. Clearly Paul Krugman and Timothy Geithner believe it. They tenaciously held to the faith while others were beginning to wilt from around mid to late-2010. What about those wilting? All those governments and their economic advisers who began preaching spending restraint from around mid-2010 when their economies were recessed with plenty of unemployed resources ready to be put to work? Are they all Keynesians still? When unemployment remained so very high, why did so-called fiscal consolidation (reducing budget deficits) become the new Holy Grail from 2010 onwards throughout Europe?

If Keynesianism works it works. If unemployment is significant, Keynesians should always explain with conviction that it would be beneficial to stimulate more, even when government debt is onerously high. They should explain that stimulus spending will produce net economic gain and a better ability to service debt. If they were convincing enough, perhaps capital markets would be supportive? And pigs might fly of course. In any event, the efforts to contain spending in Europe, in the aftermath of the post-GFC spending splurge, showed that many public sector economists had forsworn their Keynesian kit bag. It is difficult to know how many still illogically cling to the faith.

The time is right to lose the faith. This would require an understanding on the part of Keynesian economists that the economy is a complex collection of many interrelated parts, not a limited set of amorphous aggregates. Once this is understood, Keynesianism falls apart.

The European and United States debt crisis is a march of events to which Keynesianism has no answer. It has palpably failed and should be discarded. The GFC and its aftermath demonstrated its poverty. It was always poverty-stricken and enervating. Its deleterious impact was hidden by economists wielding meaningless and deceptive proofs of its success; by the resilience of market economies in the face of government economic mismanagement; and by the fact that even profligate governments take time to run down rich estates.

Toppling Keynesianism

There is recognition within economics that governments provide enormous and essential assistance to economic progress by enshrining property rights within the law. Government is seen as providing a legal umbrella within which markets play out. Government economic policy should be similarly nuanced. The guiding principle should be to provide a stable, supportive and flexible environment within which market economies, and their constituent households, workers, and firms, can prosper in normal times and, importantly, adjust in distressed times.

Politics and economics appear to go hand in hand these days. Economics should be objective. Economics is subjective in the hands of those on the left who particularly favour the interventionist character of Keynesianism. It is then not a question of whether it is right but whether it satisfies a world view that capitalism needed saving from itself by big government. The debt crises in Europe and in the United States make it evident that big government is the problem and that Keynesianism is part of that problem.

Toppling Keynesianism is essential, absolutely essential, if Western societies are to survive and thrive. Keynesianism takes longer than revolutionary socialism but it eventually does the job of leading us down the road to serfdom. Economists have an opportunity to undo the damage they have wreaked. Those in government service should consign their existing macroeconomics to the garbage bin and start reading some older texts.[33] They certainly need to build their macroeconomics around microeconomic foundations not as a disembodied artefact. As hard as that all is, unless it is done, toppling Keynesianism might be like toppling socialism. Lazarus-like it will keep popping back up.

It is important to understand the problem. Keynesian conventional wisdom has at its disposal a powerful defence mechanism in the form of national accounts and macroeconomic modelling. It has worked fairly effectively to bullet-proof Keynesianism from the march of events. The next chapter looks at this defence mechanism and how truisms become evidence in favour of Keynesian quackery. Before coming to that, a brilliant book, by Tom Woods,[34] provides an appropriate conclusion to this chapter.

---

33 See in particular Steven Kates, "Why your grandfather's economics was better than yours: On the catastrophic disappearance of Say's Law", *Quarterly Journal of Austrian Economics*, Vol 13, No. 4, Winter, 2010.
34 Thomas E. Woods Jr., *Meltdown*, Regnery Publishing, 2009.

Conclusion

Woods takes an uncompromisingly libertarian perspective to the GFC and its aftermath. Inspired by the economics of the Austrian economists, Ludwig Mises and Friedrich Hayek, he absolves capitalism and blames the GFC, and other past financial and economic crises, on currency debasement. This being the practice of central banks in promoting an expansion of credit way beyond real savings, which he sees as akin to the rulers of yore clipping gold coins. He argues that this produces untoward increases in asset prices which eventually must fall and trigger a crisis.

Woods goes on to argue that conditions, which cause crises in the first place, are logically not the ones governments should try to engineer to cure crises. In other words, credit expansion fuelling investment in unwanted assets, is best not cured by more credit expansion, bailing out failed companies and capricious government spending.

Now I don't quite see eye-to-eye with Woods in putting absolutely all of the emphasis on credit expansion in causing recessions. I also see the potential need to engineer lower real interest rates (nominal interest rates less expected price inflation) once a recession has occurred. But these are quibbles in the overall scheme of things. Woods' argument is a tour de force of logic and sense. The fact that most economic commentators don't get it obviously annoys and frustrates Woods and he lets it show. He gives special attention to *The New York Times* (*NYT*) and *The Washington Post* (*WP*). On spending bringing prosperity no matter on what it is spent: "Anyone who buys an absurdity like this belongs in a lunatic asylum or on the editorial pages of the *NYT*". On the financial bailout: the *NYT* "lived up to its usual level of sycophancy" and carried on "being wrong on everything". In comparing the GFC with the Great Depression he observed that in 1932, "as usual the quacks prevailed". He is particularly scathing of those who learnt nothing from it. "From the point of view of the geniuses at the *NYT* and *WP*, this history [the New Deal's prolongation of the Depression] may as well not have occurred." Nobel Prize winner, and unabashed Keynesian, Paul Krugman, is also in Woods' firing line: "If we want a repeat of those [Great Depression] years or if we'd like to share the fate of Japan for the past eighteen years, we should listen to Paul Krugman and implement the same policies that gave the world these two disasters."

Woods incredulously asks why governments and their economic advisers believe that spending taxpayers' money willy-nilly on misdirected and unsustainable spending will solve economic problems. In fact, this is a mystery which can be understood only by reading the macroeconomic section of first year economic textbooks or by the almost insurmountably turgid task of reading Keynes' *The General Theory*. Both tell a fictional tale of the economy being comprised of amorphous aggregates. In this aggregated world no heed is paid to resource allocation; to distinguishing between productive and unproductive investment; or between spending and production. Thus, spending on whatever will translate into production. Production of anything is good. No wonder Woods gets mad; everyone of common sense should get mad. Woods calls Keynes one of the 20th century's "crackpots". An apt term I have been happy to purloin.

11
Dressed Up Statistical Nonsense

There are three kinds of lies: lies, damn lies, and statistics.
(Benjamin Disraeli)

If there were any doubts about the potential use of statistics for fraudulent purposes, public sector economists wielding the national accounts and macroeconomic models settle the question.

National Accounting Fiction

When governments announce that GDP has risen by such and such an amount, or that consumers are spending more or less, or that businesses are investing more or less, they are using numbers provided in the national accounts. Modern national accounts mirror Keynesian theory. Demand in the form of expenditure aggregates (residential and non-residential construction spending, business investment spending, consumer spending, government spending and so on) is on one side; production on the other. Any increase in a particular expenditure aggregate is shown dollar for dollar as contributing to gross domestic product (GDP). Emphasis is placed on the contributions particular expenditure aggregates have made to production. Spending is the *sine qua non* of performance.

Most analyses of national accounts appear to lack insight as to how they are put together. Politicians usually have a story to spin and don't understand the accounts anyway. Economists should provide an insightful view. That simply doesn't happen.

Economists in and outside public service are prone to interpret the national accounts at face value and ineluctably report that Keynesian stimulus spending has worked. The accounts provide no such evidence. It is a mirage. A dollar spent by government will always be shown as contributing a dollar to GDP in the period it is spent. And, it would be shown this way even if the whole dollar were spent on imports and did not, in fact, contribute to GDP.

Money flowing through the economic system is fungible (you can't tell one dollar from another). So, was that particular dollar spent on imports or home produced goods? There is no way of telling. If the dollar were spent entirely on imports, the national accounts would show a contribution from domestic expenditure and an offsetting negative contribution from imports. There would be no way of determining that the dollar in question was the one spent on imports. Even if there were, the accounts would still be presented as they are.

The fact that government expenditure is shown dollar for dollar as contributing to economic growth is meaningless. It is a truism because of the way the accounts are constructed. It doesn't show that the stimulus spending packages work at all. It simply reflects the way the national accounts are constructed.

A pointed example demonstrates the case. Take one: government spends taxpayers' money to build a school library, at a reasonable cost. Take two: the same library is built at an inflated cost. Take three: the library having been built at an inflated cost is immediately blown up and demolished. Which of the three takes would be recorded as having a greater contribution to growth? No prizes for guessing that it is "take three", with "take two" running second. And there is more.

If in fact government takes resources away from the private sector, which might have used them productively, and uses them wastefully, this will be recorded, and written up, as the economy being saved from a decline in private sector activity by government spending. The national accounts occupy a Pollyannaish world where every piece of wasteful public expenditure adds to an economy's wellbeing. Only a moment of thought is required to see how puerile and tautological it is to say that stimulus spending works because a rise in government expenditure is shown as a rise in government expenditure in the national accounts.

In constructing and giving currency to baseless interpretations of national account figures, public sector Keynesian economists are complicit in a deception which self-servingly supports their damaging and destructive policy advice. Economists and economic commentators in the media who go along with this deception are at best, to be kind, misguided. A rudimentary understanding of the national accounts as taught in any basic economics course is all that is required to interpret the numbers properly and bring some clarity to the economic debate.

Unfortunately, the national accounts are only part one of the obscuration of the economic debate. Clarity suffers still more and ever-greater spin and deception is promulgated when public sector Keynesian economists turn to their macroeconomic econometric models.

Macroeconomic Modelling Fiction

However complex the macroeconomic models used by public sector economists, they will be based on the textbook Keynesian identity that aggregate private consumption spending plus private investment spending plus government spending plus (exports minus imports) equals production (GDP). They will also have a multiplier[35] within them showing that one dollar of expenditure adds more to production

---

35 The multiplier was introduced into economics by the English economist R.F. Kahn in 1931 and adopted by Keynes. It simply says that one dollar of expenditure will be income to someone who will in turn spend a proportion of it. The recipient of this proportion will in turn spend a further proportion and so on. The result is that the initial dollar of expenditure will give rise to some multiple of the dollar in income and production. A common estimate for the size of the multiplier is around 1.5. So $1 of expenditure is assumed to add $1.50 to income and production. Savings, taxes and leakages of expenditure into imports dampen the size of the multiplier.

than the initial dollar and a positive relationship between an increase in production and an increase in employment.

If an increase in government spending is imposed on these models they will inevitably show an increase in production and employment. It is singularly important to understand this. Whether total employment rises or falls, the models will still show that an increase in government expenditure has contributed to employment growth. This can be illustrated in stark terms by again comparing the (false) claims of both the United States Administration and the Australian Government, in the face of wildly different economic experiences.

The United States Administration claimed in mid-July 2010 that its stimulus package, rushed into law on 17 February 2009 for "shovel ready" jobs, had created or saved three million jobs. At about the same time the Australian Government claimed that its stimulus package(s) had created or saved 225,000 jobs.

These jobs in the United States and in Australia were not physically surveyed and counted, and assessed as to whether they represented net gains. They fell out of macroeconomic models. In fact, overall employment had fallen in the United States by over 2.3 million jobs (from the end of February 2009 until end June 2010). Job numbers by contrast had risen substantially in Australia during the same period. This contrasting outcome appeared to be of no consequence for those with a story to tell about the wonders of fiscal stimulus.

Employment fell in the United States yet the stimulus apparently worked to create and save many jobs. Employment grew in Australia and the fiscal stimulus worked to create and save many jobs. The United States Administration later went into overdrive immediately preceding the 2010 mid-term Congressional elections by claiming that its stimulus had averted another Great Depression. So the same glowingly positive story is told of the effectiveness of each stimulus package, even though the outcomes are quite different and opposite.

To reiterate: employment falls; employment rises; it doesn't matter one jot, the stimulus is reported as having worked. At least Christina Romer, the then chair of the White House Council of Economic Affairs, when announcing the unbelievable gain of three million jobs, had the grace (to my eyes at least) to look painfully embarrassed.

There is no basis at all for thinking that stimulus spending created anything remotely like the number of jobs claimed by either the United States Administration or the Australian Government. They are complete fabrications and fictions. Macroeconomic models cannot be used to show that a specific amount of government expenditure will or has created a specific number of jobs.

Statistical Pitfalls

Most students of statistics are given intended humorous examples of the pitfalls of drawing conclusions based on correlation. For example, figures on the increasing numbers of bankers and rising crime on the streets. These kinds of examples illustrate the silliness of mistaking correlation for causation. Yet all statistical models, however complex, must still rely on time-series or cross-sectional data and the measured correlation of particular variables, one to the other, to point to the possibility of causation. There is no getting away from that. Either it is known absolutely that one thing causes another; for example, that heat applied to water in sufficient quantities causes water to boil, in which case statistical models are redundant. Or, causal factors are unknown and statistical models juggle correlated variables to try to show what might cause what and by how much.

Social scientists are well aware of the pitfalls of modelling and the risk of reaching false conclusions. For example, two variables can appear to be causally related and yet, in fact, be both related to a third factor and be simply fellow travellers responding in lockstep to that third factor. In that case, the causal relation may appear to be robust when it is in fact non-existent. Out of sample estimation is particularly fraught.

There is no way of knowing that a relationship measured over data stretching into the past will have any explanatory power in the current period or in the future. For example, there is no doubt that GDP and employment in the United States and in Australia over, say, the last ten and twenty years, have grown in close tandem, as have GDP and government expenditure. Plug in an increase in government expenditure into models based on these correlated relationships and they will churn out a specific rise in employment. This is a modelling fiction. It has no relationship with actual experience. Yet this modelling counterpart to the movie industry's CGI is precisely what governments and Keynesian economists ask us to swallow, as though we are all as gullible as they are. If it is swallowed, the Keynesian conventional wisdom survives any march of events. If total employment falls then Keynesianism has saved jobs and prevented things from being worse. If overall employment rises then Keynesianism has created jobs and rescued the economy from recession.

It is not simply that macroeconomic models are incomplete, though that is true. They cannot capture or model all of the negative and disruptive effects of increases in government expenditure on private sector activity. It is that macroeconomic models are unfit – totally unfit – for the purpose for which they are employed. They cannot provide any guide at all to the contemporaneous effect of any piece of expenditure on employment. If they are misused for this purpose (as they are) they will always provide the same answer no matter the circumstances. They are built so as to provide an answer in keeping with the claims of Keynesian policy, while all the time being held up as providing useful information on the success or failure of that policy.

When President Obama claimed that his stimulus package would prevent unemployment from rising above 8 per cent, he did not make this up. It came from his economic advisers who used their model to conjure their prediction; and "conjure" is the right word.

Public sector economists have long perpetrated this fraud on the governments and populations of Western societies. It is a disgrace of massive proportions. It speaks poorly of a substantial part of the profession. Carry the same quality of advice across to military affairs and all wars would be lost. That would be harder to disguise.

Keynesian Quackery

Keynesianism is an undisprovable theory. The outcome can always be construed to show that government expenditure has created growth and jobs. This fiction can be countered only by conservative economists. Where are they? Well they are clearly not advising governments; they are mostly in academia as threatened minority groups or in conservative think tanks. They are needed in government to prevent every country eventually going down the Greek road to ruin and worse.

Macroeconomic models use numbers of interrelated equations and data from the past. At their clumsy best, they provide some proximate insight into the relationship between different economic variables, on average, over lengthy periods in the past. They cannot be used for explaining what has happened over any short period of time. They cannot be used to predict the future. They cannot be used for these purposes because they cannot hope to mirror the complexity of the economy with its many different demands and products. In a Keynesian world these complexities are seemly absent. It is a world of aggregates. The concept of "aggregate demand" litters all pronouncements of public sector economists. The problem is that the actual world isn't the Keynesian world and it isn't the macroeconomic modelling (CGI) world.

The misuse of the national accounts and macroeconomic modelling not only results in complete fiction being put on the public record, it bullet-proofs the Keynesian conventional wisdom against the march of events. It does not matter what has happened, good bad or indifferent, Keynesian quackery is given an undeserved tick by the national accounts and macroeconomic modelling.

Conclusion

There is hope. It is an important chink in the armour when those predisposed to the application of Keynesian remedies lose their appetite for them. National accounts and macroeconomic models are backward looking. They don't help when governments and public sector economists become fearful of the future impact of reapplying their Keynesian quack remedies. This is why the post-GFC period may turn out to be propitious for killing off Keynesianism once and for all and putting economics onto a sounder non-Keynesian footing. It is best to be cautious though. Keynesianism has been embraced by those on the left and will be protected.

Being embraced by the Left is a good clue as to why Keynesianism miserably fails economic tests. In general, good economics is incompatible with socialism in any of its forms. The next chapter begins a branch out from economic business cycles to the application of economics within a wider political context by looking specifically at the contradiction in terms involved in practising economics and socialism.

12
Contradiction in Terms

A contradiction in terms is "a statement or group of words associating incompatible objects or ideas". (A good example is a socialist economist).

Socialism is about subjectively sharing the spoils of production. Economics is about making the spoils out of which their distribution objectively falls. They are incompatible.

Personal Hayek Epiphany

In keeping with my upbringing, I started tribally on the left of the political spectrum (Chapter 1). My political position survived an undergraduate economics degree. If I had not studied economics at a postgraduate level I may have remained on the left.

Epiphany you might think is too strong a word to use in explaining a change in political and economic thinking. However, I think of it that way. Hayek gave me the insight and inspiration to question and reformulate where I stood. I am grateful for that because there is no doubt in my mind that the so-called economics of those on the left is a guide to impoverishment and despair and that good economics (which is synonymous in my mind with conservative economics) is a guide to prosperity and hope.

At some middle point in my postgraduate studies I found that my economic thinking was increasingly coming into conflict with my advocacy of left-wing arguments even though, in keeping with a university environment, I continued to prosecute them with vigour.

I took my concerns to my supervisor Professor Geoffrey Harcourt. Professor Harcourt, though on the left, is a true liberal scholar of the old school. He is now part of a declining species, I suspect. He generously and open-mindedly suggested that I read Hayek.

I did not go at first to *Road to Serfdom*, thankfully, because as justifiably famous as it is, it is (I think) a somewhat turgid read. I went to a later book, *Studies in Philosophy, Politics, Economics and the History of Ideas*.[36] It changed my economic view. And, by weaving economics and politics together in a consistent way, it also led me to the view that it is not possible to be both a socialist and an economist; at least not at the same time. Being both would be a species of Orwellian "doublethink"; of coincidently believing in conflicting stories. On the surface this doesn't make much sense. Surely there have been (and are) many learned and respected left-wing economists. Well, such people may be extremely intelligent and know a lot about economics. They might even have won Nobel prizes (like Paul Krugman and Joseph Stiglitz[37]) and be acknowledged as notable economists. Nevertheless I contend that they are not being economists when they are being socialists.

Doing Economics

Professor Joan Robinson when asked to define economics quipped that economics is what economists do (Chapter 1). Doing is important. There is an important distinction between knowledge and its application. Take a civil engineer who knows a lot about the science of building a stone self-supporting arch but, believing in levitation, insists on actually building arches which defy the underlying science and fall down. Take a doctor who knows everything about modern medicine but insists on prescribing homespun remedies handed down

---

36 F.A. Hayek, *New Studies in Philosophy, Politics, Economics and the History of Ideas*, Routledge & Kegan Paul, 1978.
37 For an account of what not to do to put America back to work, see Joseph E Stiglitz, "How to put America back to work", *Politico*, September 7, 2011.

by her dear old grandmother. Knowledge is clearly not enough; it's the doing that counts. Professor Robinson was right about that, even if unconsciously.

The role of prices is the standard bearer within economics (Chapter 2). There is nothing else within economics which is as pervasive and fundamental. It follows from this that an economist to be an economist, that is to be doing economics, must understand the role of prices; must always take that role fully and explicitly into account; and must understand the consequences of putting obstacles in the way of prices working to bring demand and supply into balance. Take this away and an economist becomes like the dodgy arch builder and doctor.

Doing Socialism

What does a socialist have to do to be a socialist? The question is whether there is within socialism a standard bearer to compare with prices in economics. State intervention to alter the outcome that free markets would otherwise produce is central to all forms (and degrees) of socialism and seems an appropriate standard bearer. Would everyone agree with this way of putting things? Probably not. Disagreement is endemic among socialists and economists. It is, nonetheless, a reasonable framework to assess whether economics and socialism are in conflict and, therefore, whether being an economist is in conflict with being a socialist. A number of examples of state intervention will be considered to make the case that doing economics and doing socialism don't mix. The first is price setting.

Price Setting

One job of free market prices is to ration demand. A common way that the state intervenes is to set artificially low prices for particular products.

Rationing demand by market price means that some who want a particular product are unable to buy it, because its price is too high. If that product is a Lamborghini, a holiday in the Royal Suite in the Burj Al Arab in Dubai, a Valentino suit, a Tiffany diamond bracelet, a manicure, or tickets to a heavyweight title fight, rationing by price is not contentious. No-one objects. Contention arises for things like medical supplies or services, education services, shelter, and child-minding. There is a view among some that these products should not be rationed by market prices. There is a view among some on the left, that some products, like medical services, should not be rationed at all. This view is plain silly and leads to unrealistic expectations. It is delusional.

The truth of the matter is that no existing society could get close to affording all of the medical services that would be demanded if their price were zero; not faintly close. The same applies to products such as education/housing/child minding. Rationing has to occur in some way. If that way is other than by market price, experience shows that it leads to nepotism, cronyism or corruption, or to just plain and simple unfairness.

A child minding place frees up in the local centre and two neighbours approach the child centre manager. First situation: one neighbour cannot afford the cost; the other can and takes the place. Second situation: neither can afford the cost (or both can); one is given the place because he knows the manager's second cousin, or is of the same religion as the manager, or was born in the same town, or belongs to the same club, or gives a kick-back to the manager, or is the better looking.

The question here is not which of the two situations is more disreputable and less consistent with a harmonious society. The answer to that is obvious. It is whether an economist, as an economist, has any role to play in deciding who should get the child minding place if the second situation applies. Quite clearly the answer is no.

An economist should bow out, having drawn attention to the possible economic implications of fixing markets. Moreover economists ought not to be promoting such non-market price arrangements. They are out of their depth. Socialists would be quite at home in dealing with the arrangement. It is part of what they do: intervening in markets to provide subsidised products to sections of the community they perceive to be disadvantaged.

Usually provision of a subsidised product is subject to an arbiter. Take public housing: who should get the house, the single mother with two children who has waited six months, or the single mother with one child who has waited 12 months? Economics and economists have nothing to offer here.

If non-market price rationing is to occur, an economist can point out that the rationing process will lead to windfall gains for some and losses for others; that it may have ripple effects on other markets outside of the rationed market; and that it may even have taxation and/or interest rate effects. Other than that, economists as economists can offer no guide on the overall impact of the outcome and therefore cannot promote the process. Economists need to talk their book. They need to make the point that rationing by market price has an openness and predictability about it that other means of rationing do not have. This is not to say that non-market price rationing should never occur; only that economics has little to say on its merits. It may well be that other disciplines such as sociology and psychology have something valuable to say. Maybe socialists who promote such arrangements should ensure they have qualifications in sociology and psychology rather than economics.

If a product is to be delivered at a market price, economists can look at the likely response of supply and demand, on the effect on substitute and complementary products, and assess the impact and merits of the proposal. The difficulty of assessing a proposed subsidised product (to be delivered below cost and below a market price) is that there is unlikely to be any hard information on who exactly will pay for it; and no hard information on who will obtain the service and on what basis.

Price ceilings have often been applied to housing rents. The result of this is to reduce the future supply of rental accommodation. Less becomes available and queues form. Allocation is based on arbitrary criteria and corruption often follows. Honorable exchanges are replaced with tawdry deals. People on both sides are lulled into acting with impropriety.

Socialists might promote non-price rationing arrangements to allocate scarce goods and services. Whatever the merits, and likely demerits, of such arrangements those promoting them should not disguise themselves as economists.

Wage Setting

Wages are the price of labour. As within any price, danger lurks whenever governments talk about doing something about them. Whatever they do will be harmful.

Influenced by a noble sentiment, to protect workers' rights, many governments have fallen for the socialist agenda of setting minimum wages. It seems like a good idea. Set a minimum wage to protect workers. It is a pity about the consequences. Minimum wages put people out of work who otherwise would gain the dignity and hope that comes with being employed and self-reliant. Of course, those who set minimum wages feel very good about themselves. After all they have protected vulnerable employees; even if that means putting some of them out of work. Labour unions favour minimum wage laws. They represent the employed. No-one represents the unemployed; except the welfare lobby.

The complexity of modern economies means that it is easy to

avoid seeing the consequences of minimum wages. In any event, those setting minimum wages don't look very hard. In a rude state of society it would be easy to spot the consequences. A worker on an island wanting ten coconuts an hour, though picking only nine while others pick twelve, would be out of work without much ado. Everybody on the island would know why.

One interesting argument in support of minimum wages is that they encourage people off welfare into employment. If wages are too low it is argued people will be less inclined to get off welfare. This really turns reality on its head. Minimum wages are often responsible in the first place for reducing employment opportunities for low skilled people and pushing them into the ranks of the long-term unemployed. Employees are best protected by a competitive market place for their services. Economists know this; or they should. As a separate but telling point, conservatives also have faith that people would prefer the dignity of work and the opportunities this brings for advancement rather than being relegated to the ranks of the unemployable as a result of socialist sanctimony.

Regulating

There is a whole lot of government regulation that in principle is not contentious. For example, few would question the need for measured regulations governing employee safety, the employment of children, protecting the environment and preventing predatory or collusive business behaviour. Problems can arise when regulation attempts to pick winners by rewarding some businesses and impeding others; or when it puts time-consuming and costly obstacles in the way of business development. It is often a judgement call as to whether this or that piece of regulation is good or bad. At the same time, it is much more likely that a socialist would turn to regulation than an economist. Financial regulation provides a contemporary case study following the ructions of the GFC.

The GFC led to a broad clamour for stronger financial regulation. This was expressed in terms of imposing additional capital and/or liquidity requirements on banks and imposing or increasing (depending on the jurisdiction) regulatory requirements on certain categories of near banks (non-bank financial institutions). It was agreed internationally to impose higher capital requirements on banks with a phase in period. It could have been much worse if the mood in the immediate aftermath of the GFC had held sway. There were calls for a range of regulatory burdens on banks and near banks, and even controls on how much banks could pay their executives. No-one sheds tears over overpaid bankers. However, if overpayment becomes egregious it should be handled by shareholders not by government. Once governments start controlling private sector pay levels, a giant leap will have been taken into dangerous socialist waters – from treading water now to gasping for air.

The clamour for imposing additional capital and liquidity burdens on banks, and on near banks, went on despite experience pointing to such measures being comparatively useless and counterproductive. They are comparatively useless because, as I have previously explained, the business of banking always leaves banks and near banks susceptible to deep recessions. This is the case whatever their capital and liquidity positions.

In deciding on financial regulation it is necessary to dispense with the trivial and the obvious. First, if financial crises are due to human greed nothing can be done about them, unless evolution does some magic. Regrettable as it might be, greed is endemic and incurable. Second, if legislation, like the *Community Reinvestment Act* in the USA, encourages poor or cavalier lending practices then clearly the offending legislation should be repealed.

This leaves the substantive matter of the required degree of prudential regulation and oversight of banks. This is not contentious in principle. There is a compelling view that there should be a set of relatively "undoubted" financial institutions to underpin financial intermediation. Financial intermediation and maturity transformation (borrowing short and lending long) are indispensible to the economy. If financial intermediation and maturity transformation are to work well, it is important to have a category of financial institutions, called banks, which are more or less beyond doubt. This allows them to gather the savings of the community, including savings of the financially unsophisticated. And most people fall into that latter category.

At the same time, it is necessary to have a spectrum of risk in the financial system to accommodate risk takers. This applies on both the saving and borrowing side. Near banks: investment banks, merchant banks, finance companies, and the like, grow to fulfil this need. A well-functioning economy must support risk taking if it is to grow dynamically. Taking risks is the counterpart of innovation and growing prosperity. It is misguided to think that everything must be safe, secure, and predictable. That is a recipe for stagnation.

Left to itself, the financial system evolves to cater for different risk appetites. However if sizeable banks go under and take savings with them it is usually far more traumatic to the economy than if a near bank fails or a major non-financial corporation fails. Accordingly, there is social and economic benefit in putting prudential safeguards around banks to lessen their susceptibility to economic downturns. As in most things, a balance has to be struck. Economists are guided by the price system in striking that balance and also in deciding how to deal with near banks and the riskier end of financial intermediation.

The character of the balance is that banks need to be as safe as practical but not so hamstrung that they occupy a small place in the financial sector compared with their near bank competitors. That would defeat the purpose. It would be counterproductive.

How about near banks? Near banks grow to escape the regulation applying to banks. More regulation on banks will lead to the relative growth of near banks. Regulation of near banks will lead to the growth of near-near banks. Where does it end? It doesn't. The conclusion is that it is futile to try to extend banking-style regulation beyond banks because institutional structures will adapt to stay ahead of the game. Moreover, forcing the system to develop new tiers of institutions simply to escape regulation has all the appearance and reality of being inefficient.

There is no science behind how much prudential regulation should apply to banks. To that extent it is not possible to say categorically that any prevailing regulation is too light, too heavy or just right. However, it is sensible when contemplating the need to strengthen regulation to take the most straightforward path in remedying whatever is considered to be amiss.

Whatever else was underlying or complicit, the GFC stemmed from banks making poor quality loans. This had nothing at all to do with the laxity of regulations in the form of capital or liquidity requirements. It was an example of what can happen when bank boards and bank regulators are derelict in performing their duties, even if they were cajoled into recklessness by government regulation via the *Community Reinvestment Act*. Perhaps they were lulled also by a long period of prosperity. Those among management, originating bad loans, which they surely must have known or suspected were bad, may have gained comfort from being able to securitise and sell the loans, and pass on the risk. Those that bought them and diced, spliced and sold them were clearly incompetent (to be generous). Incompetence like greed is abundant and will not be remedied by imposing capital and liquidity requirements. The answer is to look to better and more alert prudential oversight, rather than to new or more onerous regulations or to an extension of regulations to a wider set of institutions.

Banks have a responsibility because of their position in the financial system of not systematically originating bad loans, and packaging and on-selling them in the form of junk securities. They also have a responsibility to apply due diligence when taking assets onto their balance sheets. This goes beyond simply accepting rating agency scores. Anyone can do that. Bankers are paid to do more.

None of this is rocket science. Bank auditors have a responsibility. Bank boards have a responsibility. Bank regulators have a responsibility. They all have a responsibility to be better than fair weather scrutineers. If making poor lending decisions is the problem, then more forensic bank auditors, more diligent bank boards and more alert regulators are needed to ensure, within practicable limits, that the assets banks originate, or sell, or take onto their balance sheets, are not junk.

In part, the issue of financial regulation was politicised by the GFC because of wrong-headed charges that the capitalist system, neo-liberalism, and as its supposed offspring – greed – were causal factors in the crisis. Economists can add value, and must add value, to the debate by reference to the price system. Equally, those with common sense – no particular qualifications needed – should point out that human greed is endemic and incurable, will always exist, and can't be regulated away.

Economists should point out that the imposition of costly and discriminatory regulations on one set of institutions will always tend to lead to the relative growth of competing institutions not so burdened. Regulation of banks leads to the growth of near banks. Regulation of near banks leads to the growth of near-near banks.

It is simplistic to think that forestalling another GFC event called for more onerous regulation of banks. This might be the remedy of choice for socialists because of their penchant for intervention. Economists (should) see that it is counterproductive to reduce the relative dominance of institutions which form the core of the financial system and which contribute to its safety. In fact, the experience of the GFC might well suggest the need for less regulation on banks in terms of imposing capital or liquidity costs. Only economists could ever reach that conclusion. There is unlikely to be any example of socialists ever concluding that less regulation might be beneficial. They would be drummed out of the collective.

Stimulating

I have covered Keynesian stimulus spending extensively, though not precisely in the context of socialism versus economics. I begin with a tale which unfortunately is not a tall one.

Once upon a time in a land down under a retired rock 'n' roll star joined the government. He decided to give people "free" ceiling insulation batts to cut greenhouse gasses and stimulate the economy. It was, he thought, a win-win. If you had a roof space, even if it was already replete with batts, you could have new ones free of charge. Things did not quite work out as planned. Fly-by-night installers with no experience or expertise harassed people to agree to free insulation, even if they didn't want it and would never have paid for it. People were electrocuted and houses burnt down due to faulty installations. The regular ceiling insulation industry, not wanting to miss out on this bonanza, stocked warehouses with millions of batts imported from China (where else). It was caught short and almost destroyed when the scheme was abruptly closed down.

Pull the other one you might say if you were not in Australia in 2009. No, it is all perfectly logical in a socialist world. Collectively we have the knowledge and power to solve problems. Therefore we have a duty to act. Keynes fits snugly into this world.

Keynes laid the basis for the development of an economic recipe for action to combat recessions. He brought economic authority into a powerful coalescence with the moral imperative to act. This is a powerful combination. It resists any evidence that it is misguided and damaging. It satisfies the socialist predilection that public spending is inherently virtuous, and that capitalism needs to be periodically saved from itself.

Of course those economic commentators promoting and cheering on stimulus spending are not all socialists. For the most part, they are Keynesian dupes, simply following the script taught in the macroeconomics section of economics textbooks.

If the microeconomics and macroeconomics sections of economics texts were studied separately and then brought together when policy was developed it might not be so bad. They are not. Often economists describe themselves either as macroeconomists or as microeconomists. The latter are either useful or harmless at worst. The former are dangerous. Economists are best off sidelining the Keynesian aggregative nonsense that passes as macroeconomics. They can't get away with sidelining microeconomics. It is here that the price mechanism is brought into play.

Take the example of stimulus spending on a myriad of construction projects. This will undoubtedly stimulate the activity of builders who will purchase materials and otherwise spend some of the money they earn and, in so doing, encourage a further production response. There is no doubt about that and it is put forward as evidence that the stimulus spending works. Often this view is countered by arguments that the resultant build up of government debt, and the need to finance it, will tend to crowd out productive business investment. This is true, but economists as economists are even more inquiring.

Occupying builders on publicly-funded projects will increase building costs and make it more expensive for businesses to acquire the resources they need to expand. Government spending causes inappropriate price effects and misdirects resources. This impairs economic recovery and results in lower growth than would otherwise occur.

The implications and costs of not taking prices and resource allocation into account are twofold. First, a dollar of government expenditure is regarded as though it were as good as a dollar of business investment expenditure. Socialists obviously embrace this proposition and will not lightly let go of it. Economists do not. Economists know that resources move best when in response to price signals, not by government fiat. Socialists cannot afford to concede that.

Second, there appears to be a studied indifference about what the government dollar is spent on. It might as well be spent on unproductive projects like little used roads, school halls, bridges to nowhere, little used regional airports and pet research projects, for example, as on, say, improving stressed transport and port facilities.

When economists base their policy recommendations around the Keynesian macroeconomic part of textbooks they do a disservice to economics. Basing policy on a Keynesian topographical view of the economy is not "doing" economics. It is doing socialism. It gives imprimatur to intervention to alter the outcome that free markets would otherwise produce. And, as is nearly always the case, this particular Keynesian imprimatur causes economic dislocation and harm.

Scare-mongering

Economics is a powerful tool for looking at the world when microeconomics and the role of prices are embraced. It makes for a more informed and less scary and intimidating outlook. In this way it counters the propensity of governments to intervene inappropriately and counterproductively, based on the pretext of saving us all. Accordingly, it makes for better policymaking. "The world is running out of resources" scary story illustrates the case.

The so-called Club of Rome scared many people in the early 1970s. Frequent warnings from various conservation groups about oil and other resources running out have kept the story up to date. The Worldwide Fund for Nature is particularly prone to producing studies and issuing warnings about resources running out. In 2002, for example, it suggested that we would need to exploit other planets by 2050; and the warnings haven't stopped.

Fortunately, the world has prices and forward markets. A forward market price is the price for a resource, such as oil, in say 3, 6 and 12 months time. So there is a price of oil for immediate delivery to a buyer and a price for delivery to a buyer at some specified date in the future. Such markets exist for all important resources. The price of any resource (current and forward), and certainly those that are mined, will respond well before the resource runs out. Well before.

All mines and fields will not simply run out overnight. The available supply will start to tighten. A number of things will happen. First, the resource in question will be used more sparingly as its price rises. Second, existing substitutes will be brought more into use. Third, more efficient means of using the resource will be developed and/or new substitutes developed.

The question is whether scare-mongering and superstition are allowed to characterise and caricature man's progress and economic development as an affront to nature which will, in due course, bring comeuppance; or, whether an adult perspective is applied informed by centuries of human progress and ingenuity in overcoming difficulties. If markets are allowed to work, the price mechanism will underpin future economic development, growth and prosperity without causing too much angst. Economists know this; socialists do not. Nor do they have the slightest interest in finding out. It would cause them to question their worldview.

Equalising

Socialists are primarily concerned about achieving social justice or, equivalently, economic equity. Their emphasis is on redistributing the final product in a way that is "equitable". Equitable is a moving feast depending on some nebulous unstated criteria. Socialists see the table laden with desirable morsels. How the table came to be laden with food; where it came from and how it was grown and harvested and transported and cooked is by the way. They are entirely preoccupied with sharing. They lamely assume production will continue to occur no matter how much of the final product is confiscated and shared about.

Often those who write and talk about social justice and economic equity put production on one side and distribution on the other as detached processes. They appear to think of production and distribution as discrete and separate activities. It reaches its extreme in Karl Marx's well-known characterisation of one stage of communism: "from each according to his ability, to each according to his needs". While an impoverished socialist or communist economy might work this way, a prosperous capitalist economy cannot.

All resources, including people, move in a capitalist economy to where they get best rewarded. This means that available resources are used effectively and efficiently. Growing prosperity is the result. Detaching reward from input and attaching it to need brings down the whole system of capitalism and with it prosperity and freedom.

Economists occupy an objective place in the scheme of things. They have a level of detachment from what might be just or equitable. Their focus is on production and growth, in the knowledge that the distribution of the final product is inextricably linked with the production process. They are not discrete and separate activities. The distribution of the final product reflects the input of those contributing to production. On the whole, what someone gets out reflects what he or she puts in. Prices and wages move and adjust to produce that outcome.

This is not to say that income and wealth should simply stay where they fall from the production process. Part of the makeup of a compassionate society is to provide safety nets. These effectively redistribute income and wealth, albeit in a measured way. Three things are important. First, prices must be allowed to do their job. This brings prosperity and puts any society in a much better position to help the disadvantaged. Second, those in receipt of assistance should be given it in the form of income which they can then use to fulfil their needs as they see fit, rather than by way of market-distorting subsidies and gifts which nobody, in the end result, can make head nor tail of. Third, the economic costs of redistributing income and wealth should be understood. The next chapter throws economic light onto these costs all the way from Adam Smith.

Conclusion

Appreciation of the central role of market prices in the subject of economics distinguishes the economist from the socialist. Economists know that free markets and price movements drive economic growth and bring prosperity by rewarding human ingenuity and entrepreneurship. Economists know that the price system works. Supply and demand are brought into equality by price movements and markets are cleared. Sellers are each driven by self interest to satisfy buyers. As Adam Smith famously pointed out, "it is not from the benevolence of the butcher the brewer or the baker that we expect our dinner, but from regard to their own self interest".

The "economics" of socialism (and of those on the left more generally) interferes in market processes with the prime objective of distributing goods and services in accordance with some arbitrary and moveable equity benchmark. It fails to understand that production and distribution are part of a single complex process. It is a guide to making everyone poorer to achieve its so-called compassionate objectives. It has nothing to do with (good) economics. Economics is a powerful guide to making societies richer and therefore better able to dispense real compassion.

13
Spreading the Wealth

I think when you spread the wealth around it is good for everyone.
Barack Obama[38]

Sharing among the tribe is the hallmark of the Wantok system in Papua New Guinea. On the surface, all of that sharing seems fine but dig a little deeper and it is evident that it undermines individual effort and produces relative impoverishment. This is as true for a complex society as it is for a tribal village society. However, complexity allows those on the left to push their ideological barrow while hiding the damage it causes behind a cloak of muddled thinking.

Sharing

As a point of view, taxing the rich and spreading the wealth is guaranteed to win plaudits among the faithful on the left of the political spectrum; whether, for example, trade union or party members, intellectuals, anti-globalisation demonstrators, greens, or Occupy Wall Street (OWS) protestors. Taxing the rich to pay for improved and additional government services seems so easy and so palatable. After all who will suffer? Only the rich and they can afford it.

Politicians on the left are in thrall of taxing the rich. Most people are not rich and they have a suspicion that not too many of the rich will vote for them, even if they don't tax them heavily. It's a win-win.

---

38 Senator Obama when famously or infamously talking to Joe the plumber in the lead up to the 2008 United States presidential election.

Though, a caveat is in order. There are plenty of examples of right of centre parties following the same course. It goes further than being a popular left-wing prescript. It is to one extent or other a beguiling proposition across the political spectrum. All political parties, at times, see electoral advantage in redistributing income from the richer few to the poorer many by imposing heavier taxation on the few.

The United States is generally regarded as the epitome of individual self-reliance. It might be thought, in view of this, that the burden of tax would not be too skewed; particularly with a record of having more Republican than Democrat presidents. This would be wrong. *Internal Revenue Service* figures show that in 2009 the top 10 per cent of federal taxpayers paid a little over 70 per cent of the total federal income tax collection (compared with less than 50 per cent in 1980); while the bottom 50 per cent of taxpayers paid only 2¼ per cent[39] (compared with more than 7 per cent in 1980). And this leaves another 40 per cent of eligible voters who apparently paid no federal income taxes. This means that 70 per cent of eligible US voters pay either a negligible amount of federal income tax or none at all. So, 70 per cent of voters can support federal spending programs with little or none of the burden of paying for them. This is hardly a recipe for expenditure restraint. Nor does it fit with President Obama's constant refrain about the rich needing to "pay their fair share". Who knows what those on the left mean by a fair share? What we assuredly know is that however skewed the distribution of taxes it would be never enough.

Other countries are in a similar position. At the end of ten years or so of the "conservative" Howard Government in Australia (2007), the top 25 per cent income earners were paying a higher proportion of income tax (66 per cent) than they were at the start.[40] In the United Kingdom, it was estimated that the top 20 per cent of taxpayers pay

---

39 David S Logan, "Summary of the latest Federal individual income tax data", *Fiscal Facts* No 285, Tax Foundation, 24 October, 2011.
40 Sinclair Davidson, "Tax and Welfare", *The Howard Era*, Quadrant Books, Sydney, 2009.

a net tax rate (tax less benefits) of 33 per cent of their gross income. The poorest 20 per cent receive a net tax rebate (benefits less tax) of 32 per cent of their gross income.[41] With acknowledgement to Winston Churchill – never was so much owed by some citizens to their fellows.

It was the middle 1990s in Australia. Since 1988 a concessionary rate of tax of 15 per cent had applied to employer contributions to an employee's personal superannuation retirement savings account. This was my own, and others, path to self-sufficiency in retirement.[42] A sound and certain path you might have thought given the election of a conservative government under Prime Minister John Howard in March 1996. Not so. From August that year the new government imposed a "surcharge", not a "tax", for that would have broken a "read my lips" election promise – trickiness didn't stop with Dick. To call it as it was, a tax of an additional 15 per cent was levied on contributions to superannuation for those earning above a quite modest amount of income.

Look at it this way. With children it is hard for most people to save much when they are young and middle aged. They depend on the later years, when their income is higher and family responsibilities less, to build the nest egg. This nest egg, if large enough, allows them be self-sufficient in their retirement years and not a burden on taxpayers. This is just the personal end of it. Saving, particularly long term saving for retirement, provides the wherewithal for businesses to invest in physical capital. These investments make everyone collectively more productive and wealthier. This wealth, among other things, allows governments to raise revenue and provide welfare entitlements to those who cannot provide for themselves. It is a virtuous circle. Why then did a conservative Australian government impose additional taxes on saving?

---

41 Stuart Adam and Mike Brewer, "Observations", *Institute of Fiscal Studies*, April 2010.
42 Old age pensions provided by the state are not universal in Australia, as they are in the United States and in the United Kingdom and in other European countries. The state only provides for older people if their wealth and income fall below a specified level.

The answer is that like all governments it did so because it could get away with it. And, like all governments, it was myopic. It could get away with it because only the comparatively well off were disadvantaged. They were relatively few in number and settled in their political allegiances. It was myopic because the costs of imposing heavier taxation on saving would not be felt until much later on, well past the prevailing electoral cycle. Those future costs are twofold: first, fewer self-sufficient people, and second, a less prosperous society, because government would have commandeered resources and used them relatively wastefully. To complete the vicious circle, a less prosperous society is less able to support those in need.

Taxing the rich, and taxing them more, is apparently costless to an overwhelming proportion of the population. For example, the President Obama-inspired expansion of medical insurance in the United States in 2010 was seemingly a "free" good, if you believed, mistakenly as it turned out, that only the rich would be paying for it. Everyone knows the rich will remain rich so, in practical terms, it is apparently costless.

What has been discovered is no less than an almost never ending pot of gold. It's a form of magic; the gift that keeps on giving. The problem is there is no such thing as magic, only legerdemain. So, it isn't true. Why isn't it true? That is the question. The answer isn't of the kind usually trotted out. Adam Smith had the real answer. Before coming to that I look first at the meretricious.

The Meretricious

They will stop working so hard

If the rich are taxed too much, they will simply work less or stop working; so the tale is often told. There was a survey of motor vehicle workers in the United Kingdom in the 1960s. They were asked whether they thought their colleagues would work less overtime if the government were to increase tax rates. Over 90 per cent said that they thought their colleagues would work less. They were also asked whether they would work less. Over 90 per cent said that they wouldn't.

The fact is that the rich will keep on working because that is what they do. While this is a short and sweet answer, there is nothing else to say. Common observation is that taxation will not deter the rich from working. It will only make them work harder to avoid taxation.

They will take their bat and ball elsewhere

If the rich are taxed too much, they will take their bat and ball and go and live elsewhere. It is true that some of them will, if they can, but not so many that it will matter overmuch. For the most part people need to be where their business or employment is located. It's not easy simply to pack and move. Anyway most places that are pleasant to live in are much the same; the rich are taxed heavily. Quite simply, there are few places to go, even if the rich wanted to leave their home, which generally, like most people, they don't. No, the rich will stay around; they will work just as hard and will simply pay more of what they earn into the public purse, to the extent they can't wriggle out of it. And, they wouldn't be rich if they were not good at wriggling out of some of it.

Donald Trump was interviewed on *Fox News* prior to the mid-term November 2010 Congressional elections, when the issue of taxing the rich was prominent in the news, as it continues to be under President Obama. The question of the rich escaping to tax-friendlier foreign shores came up. In similar fashion to those surveyed motor vehicle workers in the UK, Mr Trump said he thought the rich might go and live in Switzerland, as an example of a destination of escape, if taxes became too heavy. It was pointed out by the interviewer that he hadn't left yet. Mr Trump mumbled that he might, without a skerrick of conviction.

In the United States some of the wealthy might possibly move from one state to another. The United States is somewhat unique in having state-based income taxes. Moving countries is a whole new ball game. And, even if it were to happen, it would have little impact. Factories, shopping malls, mines, real estate can't be moved. The financial wealth of the rich is already deployed without much inhibition across national borders. The amount of personal tax that any rich individual pays, however rich he or she might be, is a tiny part of the whole. It is insignificant. So if rich people leave for foreign parts, which they mainly won't, it doesn't matter too much anyway.

It will cause disenchantment

Is it unfair to tax one section of population heavily? Won't this cause disenchantment among the more heavily taxed? Strictly speaking, it may be hard to justify on moral grounds; notwithstanding the reverse argument that the rich are morally bound to assist the poor. Why should those who are especially talented, or who work especially hard, pay a much larger amount and, under progressive taxation, a much larger proportion of their earnings into the community pot?

There is biblical support for taxing the well off. The Bible mentions tithing to support priests and the less well off; for example, *Leviticus* 27:30-33, *Numbers* 18:21-28, *Deuteronomy*, 26:12, *Matthew* 23:23, *Luke* 18:12.

Tithing is 10 per cent of income. Though it adds up to a larger proportion once the priests and the poor have been separately accommodated, it is still a flat proportion. There is nothing explicit about progressive taxation in the Bible. That has to be put down as a secular invention.

While it is hard to be definitive about the moral argument, the movie *The Edge* has something useful to say. In the movie Anthony Hopkins plays a very rich businessman married to a much younger and glamorous wife (Elle McPherson). Alec Baldwin, playing none too savoury a character, at one point expresses faux sympathy for

Hopkins because of the stress his wealth must bring. Hopkins replies: "Never feel sorry for the man that owns a plane". And nor should we. The rich will manage, and resignedly put up with things, and it is best no sleep is lost over their personal plight of paying abundant taxes. It is a tyranny, of the Alexis de Tocqueville kind, of the relatively poor majority over the relatively rich minority. However it is, perhaps, the least worst of all such possible tyrannies. At least, provided it does not go so far that the hardworking are put upon by the demands of an electoral majority of the idle indigent. Unfortunately such an insufferable tyranny is not so far out of sight as to be invisible.

If the usual reasons served up as potential costs of taxing the rich more heavily are meretricious, what then is the real cost of taxing the rich? It is salutary and levelling that Adam Smith in the 18th century provided the answer.

Adam Smith

President Obama is fond of saying that the rich should pay their "fair share". Republicans respond by saying that taxing the rich will kill jobs by hitting small and medium sized businesses. Leaving partisan political posturing aside, no-one on either side, or political and economic commentators, seem to understand exactly what the costs are of taxing the rich. Adam Smith knew.

Taxing the rich imposes costs on society as a whole, rich and poor alike. It is not a free good for anyone. Economists have less excuse than others in failing to appreciate and bring into account Adam Smith's insights. Economics did not begin with Keynes.

In *Theory of Moral Sentiments*[43] Smith writes of the landlord:

> [T]hat the eye is larger than the belly, never was more fully verified than with regard to him. The capacity of his stomach bears no

---
43 Adam Smith, *Theory of Moral Sentiments*, Part IV, Chapter 1.

> proportion to the immensity of his desires, and will receive no more than that of the meanest peasant. The rest he is obliged to distribute among those who prepare in the nicest manner, that little which he himself makes use of, among those who fit up the palace in which this little is to be consumed, among those who provide and keep in order all the different baubles and trinkets which are employed in the economy of greatness; all of whom derive from his luxury and caprice that share of all of the necessaries of life which they would in vain expect from his humanity and justice.

And he goes on:

> The rich select only from the heap what is most precious and agreeable. They consume little more than the poor, and spite of their natural selfishness and rapacity ... they divide with the poor the produce of all their improvements.

It is clear that while Smith held little brief for the rich, he recognised that they did little damage and, if inadvertently (in his view), much good in the way they disposed of their wealth. Why they did little damage was because they saved rather than consumed most of their income. That is what the rich do. His observations told him that private frugality was the common inclination of those whose earnings allowed them the luxury of saving.

Brought up to date, with the most profligate will in the world, even the super rich usually have no more than a few wardrobes of clothes, six cars, four houses, a luxury yacht and a private plane. This might be excessive (some might say it is obscene even) but it adds up to very little in terms of soaking up the world's resources. It is not significant.

The rich consume little more than the poor. What an insight of Smith's that was and how it has been lost sight of. The rich save and only the rich have capacity to save very much. Consistent with this, Keynes in *The General Theory*, also pointed out that "a poorer community will be prone to consume by far the greater part of its output ...".

Savings on one side represent investment on the other; and it is investment, particularly private investment, that produces growing prosperity. Smith understood that too:

> In the midst of all the exactions of government, capital has been silently and gradually accumulated by the private frugality and good conduct of individuals, by their universal, continual, and uninterrupted effort to better their own condition. It is this effort, protected by law and allowed by liberty to exert itself in the manner that is most advantageous, which has maintained the progress of England towards opulence and improvement ...[44]

Taxing the income of the rich effectively requisitions private savings and investment for public purposes. It is not costless. It reduces private investment which otherwise produces increased prosperity for us all. While Smith had a somewhat jaundiced view of government spending – "Great nations are never impoverished by private, though they sometimes are by public prodigality and misconduct"[45] – the worth or otherwise of such spending is not the point. The point is that it is not costless when it is paid for by the rich. The cost is the product and benefit of the private investment forgone.

In fact, calls for "taxing the rich and spreading the wealth" are empty sloganeering befitting a Tammany Hall meeting. This is not because taxing the rich more than the poor is a bad idea per se. Who else can be taxed, if the poor have little? It is because the costs and consequences of taxing the rich, and of taxing the rich more, are neither acknowledged nor seemingly understood. This fools people into thinking that something can be gained without cost, and so inevitably leads to the implementation of misguided and damaging economic policy.

---

44 Adam Smith, *The Wealth of Nations*, Book Two, Chapter III.
45 Adam Smith, *The Wealth of Nations*, Book Two, Chapter III.

Socialists' Dilemma

The inescapable fact is that saving is needed to support private capital formation which, in turn, engenders future prosperity. If no-one saves, there would be no investment, even to repair the capital stock. Society would gradually revert to a primitive impoverished state. Consider the following dilemma.

Welfare recipients and those not so well off don't save very much, if anything at all. It is only the well off and the wealthy that save very much. Taxing the well off and wealthy is necessary to provide ever-increasing welfare entitlements to those perceived to be in need. Taxing the well off and wealthy reduces their capacity to save, thereby reducing investment and prosperity. A less prosperous society has less capacity to provide for the expanding welfare entitlements of the future.

Any acknowledgement of this dilemma by those on the left would be psychologically scarring. It would undermine their whole *raison d'être*. They would have to admit good economics into their worldview. They would be forced to concede the need for the rich to remain rich so that they could save and fuel economic growth, without which there would be no help for the poor. Far-sighted governments, not blighted by the economics of envy, or hamstrung by the need to finance bloated welfare expenditure on those who have no real need of it, would do all they could to allow the rich to keep and save their incomes. It is this saving that underpins private investment, economic growth, and prosperity.

None of this is saying that the rich shouldn't be taxed highly. Nor is it saying that governments will necessarily waste the taxes raised; though they undoubtedly waste a good deal. It is saying that there is a cost of taxing the rich and that this has to be taken explicitly into account. It is saying that this cost is private investment foregone which, for the most part, would have been of significant benefit because it would have been guided by market forces into satisfying real wants.

I heard a left-leaning lady say that the rich should be taxed more because they did not spend enough of their wealth. I heard this on *Fox News*. You can hear the same fallacy anywhere. People have no idea about the way economies work. That is fine so far as it goes. Not everyone can be an economist (thankfully). Unfortunately though, simplistic Keynesian quackery has seeped into the general consciousness. Spending is good. No! Saving, investment, and production are good. A great service would be done to the quality of public debate if wealthy philanthropists, like Warren Buffett and Bill Gates, began to understand that in a Western world facing a shortage of saving and capital formation, they do more good by saving the bulk of their wealth than they could ever do by giving it away to their choices of worthy causes.

Contributing to the lack of understanding about the costs of taking from the rich is the very fuzzy idea about wealth. When those on the left talk about taxing the rich and spreading the wealth it is as though they were contemplating taking money that would otherwise be under a mattress. For example, Michael Moore speaking to demonstrators during the dispute over public sector workers' collective bargaining rights in Madison, Wisconsin, in early March 2011:

> America is not broke. Not by a long shot. The country is awash in wealth and cash. It's just that it's not in your hands. It has been transferred, in the greatest heist in history, from the workers and consumers to the banks and the portfolios of the uber-rich.

This is money illusion of the kind which clouded my sister's thinking many years ago, as I mentioned in Chapter 1. Though, I should say, that in every other way I regard my sister as brighter than Moore.

Money Illusion

Money illusion is mistaking money for physical assets and goods.

Money in this particular context stands for any bit of paper or register or electronic record which claims that its holder or beneficiary owns something or is owed something. So it can refer to currency notes and coin, bank deposits, property titles, stocks and bonds. Physical assets and goods are infrastructure, residential and commercial buildings, factories, mines, machinery, and the vast array of consumer goods from luxury yachts to cars to iPods to clothes to shoes to cosmetics to bananas.

Money illusion is rampant. In fact, I sometimes suffer from the delusion that I am the only person left in the world who understands the difference between bits of paper, registers and records, which can be produced at will, with no effort to speak of, and physical assets and goods which require a whole heap of effort to produce. Certainly Michael Moore, President Obama, Warren Buffett, Bill Gates, Harry Belafonte and Sean Penn, to name just six notables, appear to have no idea of the difference. Adam Smith knew the difference, of course. Unfortunately, the economics profession, the custodian of Smith's legacy, has regressed to a more primitive state of knowledge, at least in the public domain, so far as I can tell.

Even conservative economists when confronted by the skewed distribution of financial wealth say things like: well it is a by-product of success which has benefited many people along the way by generating employment and by producing things that people want. All true. But it is only part of the story and it does little to dispel money illusion. And the most important public service of the economics profession, which it has singularly failed to discharge, is to dispel money illusion. Left unchecked, money illusion can lead to government profligacy, to social unrest, and even to insurrection, to revolution, and to communism.

The populace has a natural tendency to suffer from money illusion. Mobs, like the OWS crowd and their copy cats around the world, are besotted by it. All that money in the hands of the rich; if only it were spread around we could all be a bit rich too. They (the rich) are the reason we are not rich, because they won't share. It is all superficially beguiling. If only it were true; even I might be a revolutionary and camp outside Parliament House in Canberra, Australia, with my placard (in the summer months). It is, however, too good to be true.

Take at random some multi-millionaires/billionaires. What do they do with all that money? They spend a small proportion of it on luxuries. This is annoying for some envious types; uplifting for others who get vicarious pleasure from knowing that at least some people are frolicking on yachts in the Adriatic, even if they're not. For the most part, the rich save their money and invest it directly in productive assets or, more commonly, in stocks and bonds. This underpins the construction of buildings, factories, mines and machines which, in turn, generate goods for consumption. Progressively this engenders economic growth and widespread prosperity.

Now let's share the money around as the mob demands. Well the existing physical assets can't be spread much more thinly. Houses, factories, mines and machines can't be divvied-up very easily; and, after all, what can you do with half a square metre of factory floor. The existing stock of yachts, cars and iPods is already spread about. What will happen? Many more houses will be built and yachts, cars, and iPods made to satisfy the increased demand. This will come at the cost of investment in physical capital. The physical capital stock, which needs constant renewal, fuelled by the savings of the rich, will run down. Goods will become shoddier and in short supply. Queues will form. Economic growth will stall and start falling backwards. Misery and despotism will take the place of hope and democracy. We know all this or should do. Eastern Europe provides a recent case study.

Spreading the money makes not one additional physical thing. Yet the illusion persists and fuels dissent and worse. The OWS crowd are seriously misguided. It would be unfair to call them fools. They have been ill-served by the level of public debate and by shortcomings of economists who should have better informed that debate.

In capitalist economies, the rich mainly become rich as a by-product of contributing more than most, in one way or another, to the production of things people want. But that is just the first half of the important and valuable service they give to society. The second is that they save. Their savings underpin investment, growth and prosperity and provide the scope to relieve poverty.

We need placards saying thank you rich people (excluding government-sponsored crony capitalists); or, hooray for the one per cent! Even if it sticks in our envious craws.

Money illusion mistakes financial assets for real wealth. When people talk about spreading the wealth they have not the least idea what they are talking about. They shouldn't be given the time of day unless they explain cogently what they mean. So far that has ruled out President Obama and everybody else on the left. I explain this a little more fully below because it is so important. At the same time, I have no expectation that those in the OWS crowd or their sympathisers will ever understand.

Real Wealth

Let me re-emphasise: the only consumable man-made real (physical) wealth is already almost completely spread. The vast majority of people in Western societies own only one house, one washing machine, one refrigerator and one clothes dryer. Admittedly some may own two cars and maybe two TVs. Houses, washing machines, refrigerators, clothes dryers and even the TVs and cars, cannot be spread much more thinly to count for very much. Rich people still tend to eat only reasonable portions; as Adam Smith suggested, they did so many years ago.

Leaving aside personal and family possessions, all of the other tangible man-made wealth in the world is in the form of physical capital: infrastructure, commercial property, mines, plant and equipment, and the like. For the most part, this is fully employed making the aforesaid houses, cars, washing machines and refrigerators. There is nothing left to spread. It is important to understand this. Spreading the wealth can only mean building more houses, making more cars, washing machines and refrigerators, and so on, and distributing them to those who cannot afford them. How is it to be done? The answer is that it can't. At least it can not be done without redirecting resources and retooling factories to produce goods for immediate use and, in so doing, lessening future growth. If this simple and evidentially correct observation were more generally appreciated it would alter the whole character of political debate. The Left can be depended upon to contrive at all costs, and to spare no intellectual or logical expense, to avoid seeing it.

Financial Wealth

It is right that financial assets are concentrated. There are various estimates of this but all point to the same general picture. For example, one estimate put the top one per cent of Americans as owning 35 per cent of US wealth in 2007 and the top 20 per cent of households owning 93 per cent of non-occupied housing wealth.[46] In Australia, the top 20 per cent of households hold 60 per cent of wealth but this would be higher if the family home were removed from the figures.[47] In the United Kingdom, the top 25 per cent of adults held 77 per cent of marketable wealth in 2005.[48]

These kinds of figures are used by some to show how defective the system is: the rich have too much; the poor too little. Look at what

---

46 Professor Edward Wolff, "Recent trends in household wealth in the United States", Levy Economics Institute, Working Paper 589, March 2010.
47 *Household Wealth and Wealth Distribution*, 2005-06, Australian Bureau of Statistics.
48 *Distribution of Wealth*, 2005, H. M. Revenue & Customs.

good the rich could do if they gave their money away to the poor, you might hear it said. It is obscene that a relative few have so much when there is so much poverty. These are understandable reactions. This makes them no less superficial and misguided.

First, the concentration of financial assets is an inevitable consequence of the fact that only the rich save very much. Second, such saving provides the wherewithal to finance the building of physical capital, thereby increasing productivity and future growth. Without future growth, the availability of goods for those who are now deprived would be so much less. It is no accident that the world is more prosperous than it was, and generally grows more prosperous each year. It is down to savings and the way those savings are used to build innovative and increasingly productive physical capital.

Financial wealth – the accumulation of past savings – has its counterpart in the stock of physical capital. This stock would not disappear overnight if financial wealth were materially spread more thinly. But, it's worth saying again, because it is so misunderstood, there would be increased demand for houses, cars, consumer durables and consumer services of various kinds in future. After all, that is the purpose of spreading the wealth. This would mean less future investment in physical capital and, potentially, a reduction in the stock and quality of such capital, depending on by how much financial wealth was spread.

Without at all taking away from the benefits of philanthropy or government safety nets and even progressive taxation there is, in the end result, nothing of any materiality that can be done to relieve poverty without economic growth. Economic growth depends on investment. Investment depends on saving.

Conclusion

Leaving aside the uptick which has followed the GFC, saving has trended down over many years across most of the Western world. At the same time, only few would say that all their material wants were satisfied. Growing credit card debt is testimony to that. Disadvantage and poverty still abound to an appreciable extent. Human beings continually seek improvement in their material circumstances. Entrepreneurs and businesses continually develop new goods and services that become the essentials of tomorrow. Only savings can fuel that process. Those on the left side of politics have dealt themselves out of this process of hope, aspiration and progress. They do not have the intellectual apparatus to understand the importance of saving. Their interest is wholly concentrated on sharing the spoils of production not on its generation.

Keynesians are equally out of sync with the requirements of economic progress. They object to putting saving in the driving seat. They say that the relative abundance in developed economies means that saving is a curse rather than a virtue, and that consumer spending needs to be encouraged to maintain full employment. How many times do you see TV news applauding a lift in consumer buying as though all would be well if only everyone would spend and spend? Keynesianism is like a common sense destroying virus infecting the public debate. In the real world of households and businesses looking to their future, saving underpins economic prosperity; as Adam Smith and the later the classical economists knew it did, so many years ago.

The problem is how to resuscitate saving. Winding back the nanny state would certainly help by encouraging self-reliance. This apart, as civilisation currently stands, only the comparatively rich save in quantities. Unequal income and wealth are therefore essential to combating poverty and improving everyone's material circumstances, however much those on the left or Keynesians have difficulty in understanding that. Policies of taxing the rich more and spreading the wealth more are not necessarily ruled out by this once the consequences of reduced investment are understood. The point is that those consequences should be taken into account when such policies are espoused to make sure there are offsetting benefits of at least equal value. Taxing the rich and spreading the wealth is not a free ticket to a more equal world. Economics, properly understood, allows anyone who cares to look to see that. It is not complicated. It is not necessary to be a college professor. The only prerequisite is being free of a numbing left-wing mindset that limits objective inquiry.

The next chapter brings focus to the capacity of economics and capitalism to offer prosperity and hope as against the impoverishment and despair resulting from the application of bad economics and government patronage.

14
Hope and Despair

Calvin Coolidge [United States president during the roaring 1920s] determined that the world would do better if he involved himself less.

Amity Shlaes (*Forgotten Man*)

A news story broke in the late 1970s, I think it was. It was about three Soviet sailors jumping ship and swimming to a nearby American navy ship to seek asylum. The navies were engaged in exercises at the time. It was a ho-hum dog bites man kind of story. The highly improbable event of three American sailors jumping ship and swimming for freedom to a Soviet ship would have been more newsworthy. The direction in which people move is a telling barometer of which societies engender hope and which despair.

Hope

The French word for hope as a verb is *espérer*. Its opposite in old French was *despérer* from the Latin – to despair, to lose all hope. Hope is used in numbers of contexts which don't quite match the import of this Latin route of its opposite. Winning a lottery, flimsy hopes that the weather will be fine for a visit to the beach, and so on.

St. Paul in *Romans* had a heavy duty application of hope which matches the Latin route in import: "Tribulation produces perseverance; and perseverance, character; and character, hope". That hope is the promise of the grace of a loving God interceding on our behalf.

Economics also provides a heavy duty application on a secular plane. It is the hope that people can individually prosper and earn deserved reward by developing and applying their own talents and skills and by working hard. Properly told, economics is a guide to hope built around individuals. It must have concrete foundations; it has built great and prosperous societies.

Talk to young people undertaking tertiary education or training courses or entering the workforce in whatever capacity. It would be difficult to find many whose ambition is to live off the work of others. They would nearly all hope to prosper by dint of their own efforts. Their hope is personally energising and energising for the economy as a whole.

Economics was regarded as the dismal science. This was all Malthus' fault. He assumed that food production would increase in arithmetic progression against population's geometric progression, keeping societies on the brink of insufficiency. He was wrong about production. Man's ingenuity has been a vital part of seeing to that. The other vital part has been free markets allied with property rights. These have nurtured man's natural and beneficent inclination to pursue profits and earthly rewards. No constraint of technology or resources has yet prevented material progress. Nor will they while free markets hold sway.

Economics is in fact not a dismal science. It is, quite the contrary, a science of hope. It explains how free markets work to guide resources to where they can be best used and best rewarded. It explains how shortages are dealt with, circumvented and overcome. It explains how the savings of the most productive can be used to make everyone more productive and better rewarded. At the same time, it keeps expectations grounded. It allows anyone of common sense to understand that sharing wealth, whether justified or not, has the cost of reducing savings, investment and future economic growth. It dispels false hopes and utopian fantasies by focussing on the scarcity of resources and the constraints this brings, even when those resources are used in the best possible way. Importantly it provides insight into the despair that results when the operations of free markets are subverted. When hope in personal achievement is replaced by dependency on patronage and on the delusion that more can be shared than is collectively produced.

A combination of merit and variants of patronage wielded by government characterises the economic affairs of most societies. The balance matters. The primacy of merit is the key to hope; the primacy of patronage, the key to despair.

Merit and free market capitalism are inseparably linked. Capitalism is business Darwinism. It is an economic system which weeds out the unfit and rewards the fit and the fittest. Only merit counts. There is no moral angle to this except to say that, by definition, no other system can produce as much prosperity and, therefore, no other system allows society as much scope to support those in need of assistance; or to provide public amenities; or to support the arts; or to improve the environment; or, as regrettable as it is, to accommodate the excesses of environmentalists.

Capitalism is not a walk in the park. Adventurism, risk-taking and greed and insatiable demand for goods and services are part of the mix. This is the nature of the beast that has produced great wealth and prosperity. The alternative is relative impoverishment and, in the extreme, despotism. Set against this, the excesses of capitalism are a small price to pay.

An enormous distaste for capitalism is evident among those on the left. It has infected most of the media, Hollywood, academia and schools. It is called biting the hand that feeds you. When they look around and see well kept roads and public buildings; when they see reliable power supplies and clean water and sewage pipes; when they see prosperity in the way people are housed, eat, dress and travel; when they see people in need receiving support; when they see people battling to get into Western capitalist societies rather than to get out; they seem not to make the connection. They seem not to make the connection that it is owed to capitalism. Only free market capitalism delivers prosperity. Only capitalism is consistent with political freedom. All other economic systems lead to penury and despotism. That is why people want to escape to capitalist countries. That should not be too hard a concept to understand. A modicum of common sense and objectivity is the only requirement.

The reason no other economic system can compete with capitalism is that it operates on the margin. Businesses only grow to a point where the value they add in employing resources – particular labour and capital – is equal to the value that other businesses could add by employing those same resources. Jockeying for position is a constant theme. Businesses that develop innovative products or that can operate more efficiently, and which therefore can add more value, attract resources away from less innovative or less efficient businesses. A business that is profitable today might become unprofitable tomorrow as its competitors advance. Staying still is just not an option in a capitalist society.

What about people under this system? Are they just commodities? Well if they are commodities they are precious ones. Businesses depend on people. Businesses are forced to hire on merit; all else makes them less fit to compete in the marketplace. Businesses are forced to pay people their worth. People have the option of moving from one employer to another. People have the prospect of advancement through their own efforts and abilities. Critics might say, well does it really work like this? Isn't it the case that lots of people dislike their work and feel stuck in their job and under-rewarded? Yes it is. Capitalism isn't perfect; it simply offers the best option. It is the option which ties reward to merit. By doing that it gives people ownership of their own prospects and concrete hope in their own abilities and efforts. The alternative is reliance on government patronage.

Government patronage takes a number of forms. It is distortive when it takes the form of favouring particular businesses. Subsidising inefficient energy is an example. Contrivances by government, unions and big business to forestall uncomfortable free market competitive forces are also too often par for the course. However, free market capitalism is resilient and has, and can, survive this kind of feckless government interference. What it may struggle to survive, if it were to continue, is the insidious growth of extravagant entitlements. This has become the left's new way to engender dependency on the state, now that ownership of the means of production is largely off the agenda. This is not a conspiracy. It is simply a product of the (sharing the spoils) way those on the left think.

Sharing is good. Children are encouraged to share among themselves. The perspective is that it is a civilised and decent thing to do to voluntarily share with others. This is not an abrogation of property rights. The direction of action is voluntarily from the giver to receiver. Undoubtedly this kind of sharing has everything to recommend it. It finds adult expression in philanthropy of various kinds. It is not, of course, the kind of sharing that underpins the steep and continuing rise in entitlements. This is a forced sharing which finds its extreme expression in socialism. This extreme form of sharing is evidently best enjoyed from the outside rather than from within. Few of those on the left give away their possessions to the dispossessed and personally contemplate seeking sanctuary in the kind of sharing societies they appear to admire. Those who have ever lived within socialist societies seem to find them less attractive than do onlookers. The Michael Moores of the prosperous Western world are unlikely to volunteer to live in Cuba, while dispensing most of their wealth to the worthy poor in that particular socialist paradise.

One of the leaps that those of the left never make, apart from the leap to Cuba, is between actions and consequences. Palliative care is the forte of those on the left. The moral high ground is captured, even if it debilitates the patient. These people need assistance; give them welfare. It is a pity if that leads to dependency and despair.

Despair

A popular story of my parents when I was growing up was of a Christmas when they had satisfactorily stocked up with food, treats and presents but, both smokers, they had forgotten cigarettes. They had no money left; no bank deposit to call upon; no credit cards of course in those days; no money in a money box for a rainy day. It was Christmas Eve; there was a knock on the door. Dad was a motor mechanic for the city ambulance service and earned the odd extra "quid" on the side by working on other bloke's jalopies. It was one of those blokes with cash in hand. Dad went rushing down the street to buy some packets of Woodbines. Christmas saved!

It is, I think, a good Christmas story. For one thing, the man who owed dad money came around on Christmas Eve. He knew it would be appreciated – though not by how much – and he took the trouble. It is also a tale of contentment with the basics of life; provided cigarettes were thrown in. And, for good measure, it also provides a bridge to begin talking about measuring poverty.

There are two approaches to measuring poverty. One is based around a basket of goods and services, the other around relative income.

In the former approach, a basket of goods and services is identified representing a standard of living which provides a base acceptable level of nourishment, clothing and shelter. Those earning less than necessary to acquire such a basket are deemed poor and in need of assistance. While the basket might change somewhat as standards change, my parents' real income of 50 or 60 years ago would not fall foul of any reasonable poverty line struck on this basis. This way of measuring poverty allows the prospect of progress. There is hope in entrepreneurship, hard work, growth and development. People can lift themselves out of poverty.

In the relative income approach, the poverty line is struck where income is a certain percentage below median or mean income. This latter measure is fraught with frustration. Poverty becomes intractable unless the distribution of income can be narrowed. No matter how prosperous a society becomes, if 20 per cent of people earn less than, say, half of median income, then they will remain poor, even if they take Mediterranean holidays each year. There is no hope here in entrepreneurship, hard work, growth and development. Only narrowing the distribution of income will do the trick.

The obvious question is how narrow must the distribution of income become before a halt can be called. How much collective income and hope must be lost before some arbitrary measure of equality has been achieved. Socialism, that extreme system of patronage, sets out to make everyone's income fit within some arbitrary band whatever the cost in replacing excellence with mediocrity.

On this measure, earning 50 roubles when your neighbour also earns 50 roubles is better than earning 100 roubles when your neighbour earns 500 roubles. Equality of mediocrity is judged better than having the hope of moving up the ladder and emulating your wealthier neighbour.

That hope of moving up the ladder is a driving force that goes right through capitalist free market economies. It is not something which applies only to the intelligent, to the wealthy, to the entrepreneurial, to professionals. It applies across the board. Blue collar workers, secretaries, waiters, whatever their occupations, people in capitalist economies have around them examples of success that they can aspire to emulate; and they do. And while there are examples of corruption and nepotism in all societies, predominantly, in free market capitalist economies, merit prevails over "jobs for the boys". In capitalist economies, those who hire want the best and most productive people for the job. That is the key to successfully competing in the market place. Communist Eastern European economies failed miserably because their economic system did not allow them to compete successfully.

When workers are hired because of whom they know or whose palms they have greased rather than what they can do; when contracts are awarded through corrupt processes and under-the-counter kickbacks; and when reward is not tied to merit, productivity suffers.

Try planting a system of patronage on the sporting field where human endeavour is on view openly and without artifice. Nancy and Julia aren't nearly as good as Jill and Michele but they are put into the team because they know the coach or are second cousins to the owner. Bill and John want to stay in bed on Saturday morning so they're paid half their fee and the match played with two players short. The results of this on the team's performance would be quickly evident. It would be hard to hide. The effect of patronage on economic performance is just as devastating though, of course, not as transparent. And this is not the end of the matter. When advancement depends on patronage and ingratiation, it is the "casting couch" writ large. It sends a signal: abandon hope all ye who enter here. It demeans the human spirit and gnaws away at self-reliance.

Conclusion

Since the passing of Calvin Coolidge's time as president in 1929, governments in the United States and elsewhere have determinedly and progressively set out to help us live our lives. In other words, they have set out – well meaning or not – to make us dependent in part or in whole. Creating dependency is part of bad economics. It is a philosophy of despair. Self-reliance, the inspiring force behind prosperity, is part of good economics. It is a philosophy of hope.

Dependents form a growing constituency. It is a constituency which, at a business level, looks to government for special treatment and bail-outs; and, at an individual level, for sustenance and protection. The next chapter looks further into the pernicious growth of a cargo cult and dependency culture.

15

Cargo Cult and Dependency

> *Where they won't have to think for themselves anymore;*
> *While greedy good-doers, beneficent beasts of prey,*
> *Swarm over their lives enforcing benefits*
> *That are calculated to soothe them out of their wits.*
>
> Robert Frost (*Roadside Stand*)

Some so-called post-GFC stimulus money was given to Detroit residents in 2009. The money was provided to people who could show that they were homeless or on the brink of eviction. An interview with one recipient of this money was revealing, amusing and a little irritating; all at the same time.

Cargo Cult

When asked about the money and where she thought it had come from she said it was, "Obama money ... from Obama". When asked where she thought he got the money she said, "I don't know, his stash".

To be generous, people can be confused about where government money comes from. You might recall from Chapter 1 that my grandmother also thought the Tories had a "stash" that the British Labour Party politicians did not have.

Perhaps people are entitled to be confused, if they listen to governments and to those that want things from governments and to sections of the media. The political cacophony is all about what government has done, will do, must do, and should do. When I lived and worked in Papua New Guinea in the late 1970s, the cargo cult, though peripheral, attracted some adherents. It was based around goods coming out of the sky in aircraft and the closely-guarded secret behind this. To cult adherents, being privy to this secret was surely the key to receiving cargo. Here and elsewhere, the real key is getting the ear of government. Governments apparently can provide cargo as they choose.

This is not about the government providing and funding a range of essential or basic services, for example, defence, law enforcement, public transport, schools, a welfare safety net. It is about the multifarious and extravagant add-ons and about who pays for them.

Government can splash money around seemingly at will, as most did following the GFC. Who wouldn't want to line up, businesses and individuals (and pork-barrelling politicians), and get their cut of the stash? This is the greatest cargo cult there has ever been. This isn't a few goods coming down by aeroplane. This is billions of dollars. All apparently provided by government.

Governments are fond of claiming credit for what they spend and, in fact; often seek re-election on that basis. Up until debt becomes unmanageable there is too little partisanship in this area of political life. All political parties and governments like to spend, even if those on the left do it with more relish. It is hard to think of an example, post the Second World War, of a government seeking re-election trumpeting that it will or has cut expenditure on health, or social security benefits, or hospitals, or aged pensions, or roads, or public transport, or anything of substance? Of course they will all claim an intention to cut waste.

If ever circumstances force them into marginal cuts in benefits they huddle in defensive positions and shamefacedly blame the fates and their predecessors. On the other hand, everywhere you find governments loudly and proudly claiming credit for providing benefits without mentioning where the money is coming from. The

Detroit lady's observation and my grandmother's seem not so silly in light of this.

If governments are to be stopped from wasting taxpayers' money, the political lexicon has to be changed. Each time political parties talk about what additional amounts they intend to spend in government, they should be reminded that their intention is to spend taxpayers' money and that is the way it should be expressed. Moreover, they should be asked to estimate which particular sections of taxpayers will be footing the bill and how much they will be paying. This seems only fair. Imagine the reaction if a non-government entity were to decide to spend other people's money on numbers of schemes and not reveal who was paying what. Imagine the reaction if the schemes were fanciful and without proven economic benefit.

Dependency

In late 2009 two government ministers were reported as squabbling over soaring hospital waiting lists. Who were they? Where were they? In fact, the two ministers were from Northern Ireland, Michael McGimpsey and Sammy Wilson. It doesn't matter because it could be any anywhere.

A popular local musician went to a hospital complaining of chest pains. He was kept untreated for 80 minutes in the waiting room before he collapsed and died. Where did this happen? In fact it was Philadelphia. It doesn't matter. It could be anywhere; perhaps not entirely, because he was then robbed of his wristwatch.

In the United Kingdom, a target was set to reduce waiting time for hospital treatment to 18 weeks. Whether this target has or ever will be achieved is not the point. The point is that whatever the length of hospital queues there will be a politician promising to cut them.

In the United States, government spends more per capita on health than anywhere else. Taking public and private expenditure together, the United States spends around one-sixth of its GDP on health, as against around 10 per cent in other developed economies. That was not enough apparently. Legislation was passed in 2010 to subsidise the extension of private health insurance to another 30 million or so Americans.

Universal health care insurance was high on the agenda of the Obama administration. Why is this important? One reason is that yet more spending by the United States government puts not only the United States economy at risk, it puts the world economy at risk. Government deficit spending of the kind and magnitude that has taken place over many years in the United States and in Europe lessens prosperity by crowding out better-directed and more productive private investment. This is macroeconomic lunacy. It is also health care lunacy (posing as a moral imperative) to try to ensure that everyone has access to all of the cutting-edge health care they need, no matter their means.

In his inauguration speech, among a number of utopian pledges, President Obama promised to "wield technology's wonders to raise health care's quality and lower its cost". Anyone who knows anything about health care knows that technology's wonders have greatly increased the cost of health care and will go on doing so. Expenditure on health is a deep pit which gets deeper all the time as technology produces ever more expensive procedures, equipment and drugs, to keep people up and about and alive longer.

Quality health care, of the standard of the times, was much cheaper 50 and 100 years ago, when technology was much simpler. A promise to see that it was extended to all of the population, though infeasible then as now, was probably less unrealistic then than now.

Cutting edge medicine is incredibly expensive and simply can't be provided to everyone. This isn't a morality statement. It is a practical and pragmatic one. People have no difficulty in seeing that not everyone can be provided with a mansion. People have no difficulty in seeing that Lamborghinis are available only to the rich. Universal health care of Lamborghini standard is equally unaffordable.

There are queues for public hospitals everywhere. And everywhere politicians make promises to cut queues that they won't be able to keep. Hospital queues will always be longer than any society, however prosperous, would like them to be. Medicine will always be that kind of service that keeps ahead of any society's ability to provide its most effective form to everyone. Emergencies aside, the best rationing device, the least susceptible to corruption, is the ability to pay.

Continual improvements should be made in delivering affordable health care to as many people as possible. However, this effort should not be wrapped in false and unattainable promises and the moral indignation of utopians. Taxpayers' money should not be spent wastefully chasing a will-o'-the-wisp.

Health care is a service not an entitlement like free speech. Someone has to pay for it. No community can afford to provide cutting edge medicine to everyone who would benefit from it. Therefore some people die for the want of it and others live in difficult circumstances for the want of it. This is regrettable but the unfortunate reality is that we don't live in nirvana. The unpalatable truth is that no nation can afford to give everyone timely, top quality, health care. It would require many more seasoned and skilled doctors, many more nurses, many more hospitals and hospital beds, more expensive equipment and many more spare organs for transplanting – and the wherewithal to pay for them all. It can't be done. Just like a week's holiday in the Royal Suite at the Burj Al Arab can't be provided to everybody. At the end of the day there is no difference.

Health care is a prominent component of the growing entitlement culture: people thinking as a community that they can have things they can't afford as individuals. It forms part of the constant why isn't the government doing more refrain. Demands for higher pensions, more child-minding places, better public transport, higher welfare payments, and so on, fill the political debate. People build and buy houses in flood prone or forest fire risk areas. When the worst happens they look to their government for help. It is a rule that governments never come up to the mark; how can they? So much is expected of them. Whatever the disaster: New Orleans floods, bush fires in regional Victoria, Australia, Pakistani floods, the Gulf of Mexico oil spill, governments fail to live up the inflated expectations of their power. One news item following Hurricane Katrina criticised the lack of buses to carry people to safety. It was as though some wise authority should have had thousands of empty buses parked at the ready in case a hurricane occurred.

There is always surprise and outrage that the incompetence which typifies human and government affairs doesn't disappear once a disaster hits. Just why didn't governments do better is the lament. People invest in get-rich schemes. When the schemes flounder they look to their government to bail them out. Tourists get stuck in a foreign country because of bad weather or civil unrest and immediately ask their government for help and usually complain if that help is at all tardy in coming. The list goes on.

Government patronage over many decades has created the most unrealistic expectations of the power of governments. In an earlier age people despised the reach of government, now they snuggle into its embrace and squall if the milk and honey doesn't flow. Where is King Canute when needed?

The music will stop. Entitlements are becoming increasingly unaffordable. The difficulties should not be underestimated. If things continue as they have been, a tipping point will be reached, not too far distant, where half the populations in Western countries will be materially dependent on entitlements. OECD figures show that the proportion of GDP spent on social welfare grew from an aggregate 16 per cent of GDP across all OECD countries in 1980 to 21 per cent in 2005. This is a big proportion of GDP but these figures tell only part of the story. For example, the UK think tank *Civitas* reported in 2007 that one-third of UK households depended on welfare for half and more of their income. The German newspaper *Bild* reported in 2006 that 42 per cent of households in Germany relied on welfare payments of various kinds. Peter Saunders (*Australia's Welfare Habit*[49]) wrote that "forty years ago, only 3% of working age Australians depended on welfare payments as their main source of income. Today it is 16%. There used to be 22 workers to support each person on welfare. Now there are five". The figures have gotten only worse.

Leave aside what this does to national budgets. As important as this is, it is not nearly as important as the debilitating effect it has on welfare recipients. Entitlement spending was originally devised to help the poor and those unable to work. It is a noble cause and no civilised society would turn back to an uncaring age. But, enough is enough. It has now run amuck. It has gone far beyond providing a safety net. It has made mendicants and dependents out of people who would otherwise be self-reliant. Quite simply, it is disastrous. No end is in sight. Most politicians live off pandering to it. Voters are addicted to it. It has to be turned back, at least to some extent. The responses to the government debt crisis in Europe and the United States offer some hope. This is covered in the final chapter. Hope might also lie in grass roots movements like the Tea Party, inspiring conservative politicians to embrace good economics, whatever their past infidelities.

The Tea Party movement would have had no legs were it not for unsustainable spending, yet its objectives go beyond simply controlling government spending, towards a society which limits government and encourages and rewards merit and self-reliance. It may catch on in more cosseted European societies, although it is hard to imagine it ever having begun, or having great energy, outside the United States. Unless conservative economic values are at least partially restored in

---

49 Peter Saunders, *Australia's Welfare Habit*, Centre for Independent Studies, 2004.

the United States they will not be restored anywhere and Western civilisation, which after all represents the best that human beings have ever achieved, and are ever likely to achieve, will become increasingly enfeebled and may eventually fall by the wayside. It is as simple and as serious as that.

Conclusion

The political left builds its constituency around undermining individual self-reliance and keeping people more and still more dependent. Their agenda offers no hope. It leads to impoverishment and loss of freedom. Don't think it can't happen. It is happening. All that is needed is a few more decades of more of the same and too many will be on the public teat to turn it around. Eastern Europe had a glowingly better model on its doorstep. What happens if there is no better model, if even the United States succumbs, if it is all the same dross?

The next chapter puts dependency into an international aid setting and also looks at the issues surrounding the upsurging economic migration from poor to rich countries. While economic migration might not at first glance appear to be a dependency issue, dig a little deeper and it is evident that it has become one. It has now effectively become a case of rich countries offering economic sanctuary to those fleeing dysfunctional societies.

16
International Aid and Migration

Pakistan received $58 billion in foreign aid from 1950-99. However, it systematically under-performed on most of the social and political indicators.

Fayyaz Baqir (*Reforms and Civil Society Engagement*, November 2007)

There is an agreed international aspirational target for developed countries to provide 0.7 per cent of their national income for international aid. Only the Scandinavian countries, and Holland and Luxembourg, had met this target by 2010. Measured over all donor countries, the average per cent of national income going to aid is only around half of the aspirational target. The United States is the largest aid donor in absolute terms.

International Aid

For developed countries as whole to double their aid to reach the aspirational target would mean a massive additional annual transfer of their taxpayers' income and wealth. There would be additional demands if ever an enforceable international carbon dioxide emissions agreement were to be concluded. Though never seriously considered at the Copenhagen climate summit in December 2009, the leaked draft international treaty (*Framework Convention on Climate Change*) would have obliged developed countries to provide more massive ongoing aid to developing countries. Numbers of figures were thrown around in the draft treaty but, for example, 0.5 and

0.7 per cent of GDP per year for "adaption" appeared as options. Adaption was only one of the imperatives. There was "mitigation" and combating the impact of "deforestation" and the free transfer of mitigating technology from companies in developed countries to companies in developing countries. This log of claims remains an integral part of the climate circus.

In the December 2011 summit in Durban it was agreed that a "Green Climate Fund" will be established offering poorer countries $100bn per year (from the pockets of Western taxpayers remember) in climate aid to help them "develop cleanly and adapt to climate impacts". Luckily nothing yet is set in stone. Imagine the waste; the missing billions, the scams; the boondoggles, the chicanery, the corruption; the gaming; and the sheer unmitigated folly of helping poorer countries build windmills. Surely God must be groaning. I gave them Einstein and they're building windmills?

Demands for foreign aid and more of it have been constant since the end of Second World War. So called climate change has become yet another reason for aid. Aid, assistance to others, can generally be put into two categories: transitional aid to alleviate temporary incapacities and ongoing aid to relieve permanent incapacities.

Advanced societies provide support for their own people. They provide support to some people and families on a temporary basis and to some on a continuing basis. There is a sharp difference between the two. The original assumption was that the able bodied would only ever require temporary support. Societies didn't set out with an intention to provide ongoing support to those who can take care of themselves. The idea was to provide a bridge, even if this has now been subverted by the entitlement culture.

Where does foreign aid fall in all of this? Is aid a bridge? Alternatively, is it assumed that countries receiving aid yesterday and today will need aid tomorrow and into an indefinite future? Which alternative seems to have been the script so far? There is no evidence that demands for aid, and more aid, have any sunset clause.

There is no case to be made for never-ending foreign aid, outside of responding in neighbourly fashion to emergency situations caused by natural disasters of various kinds.

Societies have a responsibility to take care of themselves. Millions of people working constructively inside open non-corrupt societies, allowing market forces to operate within the rule of law, will achieve economic progress. Societies which are closed and corrupt will not. Providing continual aid to the former set of societies is unnecessary. Providing continual aid to the latter is pandering to dysfunctional behaviour and that is no way to bring it to an end.

Foreign aid should be given a definite life and made conditional on the societies in receipt of it becoming open, lawful, free market democracies. It is counterproductive to encourage dysfunctional societies to remain dysfunctional by continuously providing palliative care. It is to be expected that those on the left support more and continuing foreign aid. They deal in despair about the potential of achieving self-reliant economic prosperity. Economists should deal in confident hope that it can be achieved.

Economic migration

Economic migration has turned into another form of economic aid. An economist sees great value in labour moving to where it is most productive. However, the assumption is that productivity isn't being artificially depressed in one place causing labour to move to another. Effectively, this is precisely what's happening as economic migrants flee from dysfunctional societies.

A seminal moment occurred in economics in 1817. English economist David Ricardo set out his theory of comparative advantage, described by Robert Findlay in the *New Palgrave Dictionary of Economics*,⁵⁰ as the "most beautiful result in all of economics". The theory of comparative advantage demonstrates that specialisation and trade between two countries increases total output and therefore has the potential of making both countries better off economically, even if one country can produce everything at less cost than the other.⁵¹

Before Ricardo it was appreciated that trade would be beneficial between countries if each could produce a mutually desired product at materially less absolute cost than could the other. It was not appreciated that gains would still be made in circumstances where one country had an absolute cost advantage across all products. It is a powerful result. Though I doubt Ricardo, in his time, considered that the application of his theory would be shaping, and will continue to shape, the course of Western civilisation.

The world is a complex and dynamic place and economists, particularly of mathematical bent, revel in complexity. Accordingly, Ricardo's model has been tugged and pulled to try to fit it into a world of many countries, many products, different kinds of resources, and ever-changing conditions. While this is important work, and has its fascination for some, none of it takes away from or substantially modifies the Ricardian insight. This insight carries two implications though perhaps "portents" would be a better word. One is that there is not necessarily any limit to complete specialisation. In other words,

---

50 *The New Palgrave Dictionary of Economics*, Macmillan, 1987, Volume 1, page 513.
51 To partially use Ricardo's example, if because of the relative disposition of advantages, England requires two resource units (RUs) to produce one unit of cloth and eight to produce one unit of wine, while Portugal requires just one RU to produce either one unit of cloth or wine, Portugal can produce both more cheaply. However, the overall production of cloth and wine would rise if England concentrated on producing cloth and Portugal wine. To make the arithmetic simple, for each eight RUs that England switched to cloth from wine, four additional units of cloth would be produced for the loss of one unit of wine. For each two RUs that Portugal switched to wine from cloth, two additional units of wine would be produced for the loss of two units of cloth. An aggregate gain to be shared would result in two units of cloth and one unit of wine.

inside the constraint of world demand for any particular product and barring diseconomies of scale, each product will tend to be all produced in one place. And moreover, economies of scale are more likely to predominate and therefore to reinforce the process towards specialisation. The second portent arises from Ricardo's assumption that resources, particularly labour, are trapped within national borders. If labour were not so trapped it would tend to flow to where it was most productive. Literally speaking it might flow from one country to another until one was empty. This is silly of course but the tendency has force and validity and we are seeing it being played out.

International trade formed just two per cent of global output in 1820.[52]. Agriculture employed more people than any other sector. It accounted for close to 40 per cent of employment in England, by far the most advanced industrial and urbanised country of the time, and for a much larger proportion in other European countries.[53] Agricultural production, as distinct from its output, can't be easily moved geographically for obvious reasons. Manufactured goods were relatively costly to transport compared with their value. This imposed a relatively high hurdle on manufactured exports. There were no well-developed international currency and bond markets. Private financial capital was therefore largely employed within national borders. Though border controls were lax, the absence of communication technology (the telegraph had still to be invented) had an insulating effect on local populations. Different cultures and languages kept them largely at home. Industrialisation resulted in internal migration from rural areas to towns and there were seasonal cross border movements of labour in continental Europe but large permanent cross border movements

---

52 Bruce Greenwald and Judd Kahn, *Globalization: n. the Irrational Fear That Someone in China is Going to Steal Your Job*, John Wiley, 2010.
53 N.F.R. Crafts, *British Economic Growth During the Industrial Revolution*, OUP, 1985.

were largely confined to migration to the new world.⁵⁴

Now the world is quite different. International trade at two percent in 1820 had risen to 30 per cent of global output by 2000. Manufacturing production far outstrips agricultural production in developed economies which, in turn, is dwarfed by the provision of government and non-government services. Tariff walls, so long in place, have progressively fallen away since the Second World War as bilateral and multilateral agreements through the GATT have lowered and removed barriers. Financial capital moves seamlessly between countries. National borders have become effectively more porous, de facto and de jure. The European Union presents an extreme example of the latter. Communication technology has demystified alien cultures. All of a sudden, when measured in historical terms, the theory of comparative advantage has fertile ground on which to play out. And there is undoubtedly much more to come. We are perhaps only on the threshold of its influence despite the great changes it has already wrought.

The world seems to be heading in the direction comparative advantage says it will at great speed: to ever greater specialisation. This is giving Western economies severe adjustment problems as traditional manufacturing industries fall to foreign competition. In turn, this is leaving workers behind who find themselves with the wrong skills and in the wrong places. Take the United States as a representative example. Geenwald and Kahn⁵⁵ report that there were one-and-half-million well-paid autoworkers in 1970; fewer than half remained by 2007. Those employed in traditional manufacturing roles fell by 10 percent from 1970 to 2005 against an overall rise in employment of 80 percent. During the same period people working in managerial and

---

54 L.P. Moch, *Moving Europeans: Migration in Western Europe since 1650*, Indiana University Press, 2003.
55 Bruce Greenwald and Judd Kahn, *Globalization: n. the Irrational Fear That Someone in China is Going to Steal Your Job*, John Wiley, 2010.

professional roles grew by 153 per cent and in service occupations by 123 per cent.

Comparative advantage is also working to draw people from less developed countries to where they can add most economic value. People are not as trapped within borders now as Ricardo was safe in assuming in 1817.

While the issue of refugees tends to dominate the news, the dominant component of migration, which has upsurged since the Second World War and most particularly since the mid-1980s, [56]has been economic migration from poor to rich countries. Europe and the United States, of course, have figured prominently as destination areas. While the ending of colonial rule coincided with the start of migration flows to Europe, this, in itself, did not prompt migration; economics did.[57] This is illustrated by the relatively wealthy Japan, Hong Kong, Taiwan and Singapore joining the ranks of destination countries.

Economic migration has both a push and pull factor. Migrants seek economic advancement. Businesses in host countries seek labour and cheaper labour. This is all economically rational so far as it goes, but when comparative advantage is compounded by deliberate disadvantage engineered by dysfunctional societies it becomes problematic. Migrant flows have become migrant flees. People movements are presenting Western economies with cultural absorption challenges which go to the heart of their national character, while doing nothing to remedy the economic circumstances in poorer countries. In these circumstances, the only answer in the short run may be to impose much greater restrictions on economic migration, however much business lobbies in richer countries complain.

Comparative advantage has come of age in an era where tariff

---

56 Stephen Castles & Mark Miller, *The Age of Migration*, Palgrave Macmillan, 2003.
57 Christopher Caldwell, *Reflections on the Revolution in Europe: Immigration, Islam, and the West*, Allen Lane, 2009.

protection has been dismantled; where communications technology has demystified the world for even remote villagers in remote countries; where borders are porous; where developed countries have advanced to widen the gap between the haves and have nots; and, critically, where economic disparity has been heightened by the dysfunctional policies and practices of many poorer countries. Only comparatively recently have the full effects become evident. In these circumstances, restricting economic immigration serves three purposes.

First, it protects the exceptional cultural traditions and institutions of Western societies. Second, by making imported labour harder to get it encourages businesses to find ways to use home grown labour left behind geographically and functionally rather than taking the easier road of importing labour. Finally, it allows comparative advantage to play out as it was envisaged by Ricardo. Less developed countries have the scope to specialise in activities in which they have a comparative (albeit not an absolute advantage). Simply exporting labour undercuts and limits the opportunities and scope less developed economies have to develop their own competitive industries.

Conclusion

Consequences are important. Economics provides an understanding that incentives are important in causing change. Resources are shifted from one use to another in response to profitable opportunities; people move from one job or business to another in response to the prospect of higher reward. Economics properly understood also tells us that property rights and free market forces have the potential of lifting all societies from penury, of giving all societies, without exception, the concrete hope of prosperity. Providing unconditional foreign aid tends to cement dependency and disadvantage in place; and the evidence for that is clear enough. Third world countries remain third world countries unless they establish conditions in which market forces have scope to flourish.

The full expression of free markets allows goods and people to move freely between countries. However, allowing free movement of people requires a precondition that economic advantage is not skewed because of grossly dysfunctional policies and practices on the part of numbers of countries. Otherwise, economic migration becomes fleeing at levels which strain those countries providing economic sanctuary as it drains those countries from which migrants flee.

Providing aid and economic sanctuary are both part of an ethos which encourages dependency and the view that collectively one group of people can and should prop up another. Part of that same ethos is the illusion that collective action can remove economic disadvantage and solve economic problems.

The next four short chapters explore how solving economic problems has become detached from reality, reason, and achievability, in the mindset of the political and economic left. The first goes to the progressive phenomenon of being unhinged from practicality; the second to making utopian pledges; the third to bad arithmetic; and the fourth to having delusions of power over economic events. Once these phenomena take hold good economics is ignored, bad economics takes over and untold economic damage results. We see this being played out in the Western world.

17
Unhinged from Practicality

We set ourselves this first goal: by 1990 no Australian child will be living in poverty
Australian Prime Minister, R.J. Hawke, June 23, 1987.

Conservatives believe that they are more hinged to practicality than are those on the left. Casual empirical observation bears this out, though it would probably be denied by those on the left. However, leaving empiricism aside, there is reason to suppose that those on the left have more licence to roam into fantasy on a range of economic and social issues than have conservatives.

Licence to Roam

Imagine an economic model in the form of a perpendicular line on which the actual dimension of a particular economic or social problem and the optimal amount of government intervention is pinpointed, though no-one knows the precise location of the point. North of the point lies the territory of saying that problems are larger than they are and that more must be done and spent. South of the point lies the territory of saying that problems are smaller than they are and that less need be done and spent. As a simple example, take the amount of public funds that should be spent on the welfare of a particular disadvantaged group within society, say, an indigenous population.

While the optimum amount is unknown an educated guess can be made as to the likely relative positions occupied by those on the left and conservatives. Conservatives would likely emphasise self-reliance and be south of those on the left who would emphasise collective responsibility. Moreover, the dispersion of amounts among those on the left is likely to be much greater than the dispersion of amounts among conservatives. The reason is clear. Conservatives usually cannot afford to travel very far, if at all, south of the status quo. For example, to hold a position that considerably less should be spent on indigenous welfare programs is not a tenable position. It would earn brickbats. On the other hand, to say that expenditure should be vastly increased, however impractical, earns bouquets. There are almost no boundaries to the respectability of claims in that direction. This means that the left will throw up outliers (e.g., John Pilger, Michael Moore, Noam Chomsky) freed from the prosaic dullness of practicality.

There is any number of examples to illustrate the case. Public expenditure on health is always in contention. Stories about how bad the health system is (babies born in hospital rest rooms/people dying in waiting rooms) dwarf those that extol its effectiveness. In these circumstances, it is obviously easier to hold to the totally unrealistic and impractical view that everyone must be provided with first quality health care, no matter how much it costs, than it is to hold to the view that too much is already being spent. Those on the left have licence to travel far north; conservatives are anchored by the status quo and have much less scope to travel south.

Green groups in Western nations can urge that economies should be dislocated in the cause of saving the planet without too much practical limit. Politicians sceptical about man-made global warming have greater difficulty in saying that it is all bosh and that they are going to do nothing and, in fact, build more coal power stations. As an aside, it is interesting that the Chinese can have their cake and eat it too by building coal power stations as fast as they can while being climate change devotees. Western politicians appear not to have that luxury.

Church groups can urge Western nations to allow the settlement of more refugees (without specifying any limit). No mainstream politician can get away with saying that all illegal would-be immigrants should be repatriated as a matter of course.

There are cases – notably policing and defence – where the positions of those on the left and conservatives can be somewhat reversed along the north-south line. In these cases, conservatives sometimes can travel further north than those on the left can travel south. President Obama, for example, eventually decided at the end of 2009 to put more troops into Afghanistan despite his prolonged and evident anguish at the prospect.

Conclusion

Having carte blanche is corruptive. Rather like children with large inheritances, those on the left have scope to go off the rails. It becomes understandable why they might be less hinged to practicality. Seen in this light, for example, President Obama's promise to provide health insurance to 30 million uninsured Americans without increasing the budget deficit by one dollar starts to make sense.

A forlorn longing for Utopia is next.

18
Utopia

[T]here is one heresy which it seems to me that some political doctrines embrace. It is a belief that man is perfectible. This takes the form of supposing that if we get our social institutions right – if we provide properly for education, health and all other branches of social welfare – we shall have exorcised the Devil. This is bad theology and also conflicts with our own experience.

Margaret Thatcher (at the Church of St Lawrence Jewry, London, 30 March 1978)

Those on the left of the political spectrum are prone to making outlandish pledges and promises. A left-leaning friend of mine once said to me: "Well there is nothing wrong with being aspirational".

Outlandish Pledges and Promises

A good place to start is at a point of agreement among everyone of good will:

> I have a dream that one day this nation will rise up and live out the true meaning of its creed: We hold these truths to be self-evident; that all men are created equal.

This was part of an inspirational and aspirational speech by Martin Luther King in 1963. It is possible to quibble that it was unrealistic. There will always be those that will not hold those particular truths to be self-evident. However this is a minor quibble. Great progress has been made, as Dr King dreamt it would. Importantly such progress was conceivable when King made his speech. Each and every individual could by dint of their own efforts help to achieve it. This was not a call to some external agency or force, or to some collective action that individuals had little power to control. This was a call to each and every person in the United States as individuals. Each person could ask themselves the question: am I in my life treating everyone with equal respect regardless of race. And they could do something about it if they were not. This was not a call to end world poverty. Imagine what an individual can do about that. Imagine the cynicism about its achievability. Having heard a call to end world poverty, most people go home have their dinner and watch TV.

King's speech was aspirational; it was not in the least outlandish. It appealed to individual action. It contained no utopian promises or pledges. Sir Thomas More provided the road map for such promises and pledges in his book *Utopia*.

Sir Thomas More's *Utopia* described the "ideal state" of tranquillity and sufficiency. More did not believe that such a state was achievable and neither, presumably, do those on the left. But the shimmering prospect of a much better world where economic disadvantage is largely absent still drives the agenda of those on the left. When the possibility of freeing all from poverty and "outrageous fortune" is not an impossible dream there is always much to do. Inaction is untenable and, in fact, immoral.

Conservative economic thought (good economics) is really up against it in questioning this worldview. It's hard to capture hearts and minds when you question whether giving everyone timely access to good quality health care can be afforded; whether homelessness and child poverty can be ever entirely eliminated; whether the continued provision of foreign aid does anything to cure third world poverty. Nonetheless, as hard as it is, the fight has to be fought because experience shows that only modest advances can be achieved in the face of economic forces of scarcity and caprice.

Conservative economic thought is not about inaction. It is about making realistic assessments of what can be done. As such, it should not yield the moral or economic high ground to those with utopian-like visions. Such visions give rise to false hopes. False hopes give rise to disappointments. Disappointments, repeated often enough, give rise to despair.

Socialism in its more extreme form advocates government control over the means of production, distribution and exchange. These days, with the experience of Eastern Europe still fresh, and populations enamoured with the wealth capitalism has brought, the Left has generally taken on a less revolutionary face. It is now all about government taming the capitalist system to varying extents and subverting it with entitlements. Nevertheless, utopia lurks. Part of the Left's worldview is that with the collective will poverty and disadvantage can be largely eliminated.

This is not about making measured progress or about improving the lot of the disadvantaged. Everyone believes this is possible and should be pursued. It is about the quantity of improvement that can be achieved. President Obama found it possible to say in his inauguration speech that we will, "wield technology's wonders to raise health care's quality and lower its cost", and of developing economies, "let clean water flow". This was accepted at face value or at least treated with more credibility than flying saucer sightings, even though equally fanciful. Within a worldview where utopian-like progress is achievable through collective efforts, it's all perfectly possible. No-one on the left questioned President Obama's outlandish promise to make clean water flow throughout the developing world.

Free market capitalism blamed by many for the GFC would probably be regarded by Winston Churchill in a similar light as democracy: worse than any other system except for all the rest. But then Churchill was a realist not a utopian: "I have nothing to offer but blood, toil, tears and sweat", he said, though admittedly in particularly threatening times.

Those on the left believe that things can be put right and kept right if only the right amount of government is applied to the affairs of men and women. Australian Prime Minister Bob Hawke pledged in 1987 that no child would live in poverty in Australia by 1990. While this pledge was particularly unrealistic and untenable, and made to look ridiculous in short order, it forms part of a common thread of over-promising among those on the left. This applies, perhaps with even more force, in the United States. Over-promising tends to be proportional to economic and population size. It's hard to over promise, and be taken seriously, if there are a few of you on a small desert island.

Consider the extracts below: first, from President Clinton's (second) inauguration speech and, second, from President Obama's in January 2009.

> The promise we sought in a new land we will find again in a land of new promise ... In this new land education will be every citizen's most prized possession. Our schools will have the highest standards in the world, igniting the spark of possibility in the eyes of every girl and boy ... Our streets will echo again to the laughter of children...Everyone who can work, will work, with today's permanent underclass part of tomorrow's growing middle class. New miracles of medicine ... (Clinton)
>
> We will ... wield technology's wonders to raise health care's quality and lower its cost ... To the people of poor nations, we pledge to make your farms flourish and let clean water flow ... We will harness the sun and the winds and the soil to fuel our cars and run our factories. (Obama)

Now consider in contrast President Reagan looking forward in his first inauguration speech; back it seems to blood and toil.

> Can we solve the problems confronting us? Well, the answer is an unequivocal "yes"... In the days ahead I will propose removing the road blocks that have slowed our economy and reduced

productivity. Steps will be taken aimed at restoring the balance between the various levels of government. Progress may be slow – measured in inches and feet not miles – but we will progress.

Maybe utopian thinking will eventually be put aside in the light of experience. However, there is no sign of it happening any time soon. It appears to be impervious to logic and experience. If results are disappointing they are explained away. It was because of the way it was done. Next time it will be done differently and the benefits will flow.

Conclusion

The randomness of suffering and enrichment, the perseverance and striving required to earn, save and build assets, human flaws and frailties, all point to the futility of believing in pipedreams. Only when a politician promises hard work and the possibility of modest returns do they have credibility. In part, the Left's utopian visions rest on what is an "adding up" problem. It is a problem of a kind which says that if a million people contribute a dollar each there will be much more than one million dollars to spend. It's the loaves and fishes writ large without the benefit of Jesus Christ.

19

Bad Arithmetic

If the Führer wants it, two and two makes five!
(Hermann Göring)

The OECD published a paper in 1998 (*Forces Shaping Tax Policy*) which said that budget deficits and government indebtedness had risen faster than GDP in virtually all OECD countries during the previous 30 years. It noted that most of the growth in public expenditure had been social welfare spending. In 1998, the OECD-wide budget deficit was two per cent of GDP and net indebtedness 44 per cent. By 2010, the comparable projected figures were eight per cent and 58 per cent; and it has got much worse since. Governments seem to be incapable of living within their means. They have an adding up problem.

Adding Up Problem

In economics there is a concept called the adding up problem, otherwise referred to as Euler's theorem. It is an obscure theorem about the sum of the marginal products of factors of production adding up exactly to the total product. This is not about that; it is about the more prosaic adding up problem which governments have had in abundance in recent decades.

The emergence of something different and grander from the coming together of numbers of elements is not unusual in the natural or man-made world. Life is created that way. Numbers of engineering, physical and chemical processes result in something new and different being produced when elements combine or are combined. To give an example: a cathedral starts its life as rocks and sand and other elemental materials. Everyone would agree that the cathedral is more than the sum of its parts. At the same time, everyone should be able to agree that the weight of the cathedral is exactly the same as the weight of the materials combined in its construction.

Equally, if one hundred people were to combine their money (and each had $1000), they would together have $100,000. Alchemy would not convert this sum to a bigger sum. This is important. Suppose there were 50 million people each with $1000 as before. Then together they would have $50 billion. They would not have $100 billion. The mere fact of them combining their wealth would not of itself create more of it. People with any ability to count up might say: Stop! This is all obvious. Well apparently it isn't.

Nation states defy arithmetic. The bigger the state the less constrained it is by arithmetic. The whole pot of money magically adds up to more than the sum of its parts. It is as though politicians and governments across Europe and North America, and most everywhere, need remedial classes in adding up.

Why do some economists and politicians think that governments can spend and borrow more than they can reasonably earn and repay. Well the truth is that they don't. They always think they can repay it because they are blindsided by large numbers. They know as individuals that they have to live within their means. They know this applies to everyone in their country. At this point their minds must go through an Orwellian transformation where two plus two can indeed equal five; where the whole is greater, and sometimes much greater, than the sum of parts. They would know on a desert island that if each of the ten inhabitants picked ten coconuts, there would be just 100 coconuts to share. But once the number of inhabitants reaches, say, ten million, and coconuts become one of, say, fifty thousand products, everything apparently becomes possible. They are loosed from the shackles of irksome arithmetic.

One of the problems has been that Keynesian economic advisers have dominated public services. Unfortunately, as I have previously noted, conservative economists have largely remained in think tanks or as endangered species in academia. On the whole Keynesian economists are predisposed to thinking in terms of aggregates having a life of their own rather than being a collection of many components. Conservative economists think on a more microeconomic level and are therefore less susceptible to thinking that the whole is greater than the sum of parts.

On the whole, the division between those on the economic left (including Keynesians) and economic conservatives is profound. To use and evolutionary term, it is possibly an example of speciation without the benefit of geographical isolation. Two species have developed alongside each other, looking exactly the same, but thinking quite differently. One believes in the tooth fairy; the other doesn't. Unfortunately those on the left have so infected the public debate that most otherwise sensible people have bought the line.

A long list of services has morphed from being in the category of "nice to have" to the category of entitlements. A country is simply a collection of people who cannot go on forever paying themselves more than they earn. People used to understand that they could have no more than they earned. Gradually numbers of people began to understand that they could have more by having what others earned. This I describe as the infectious stage of progressive/socialist thinking. Now, an increasing number of people believe they can share more than the community collectively earns. This I describe as the terminal stage. An extremely hard road lies ahead of ridding society of this alluring (bottomless pit of gold) misconception. Giving politicians and Keynesian economists remedial classes in arithmetic might be a start.

Conclusion

Suffering from recurring economic pipedreams, constantly shattered by reality, and from endemically poor arithmetic brought to book by crippling debt, would be salutary for most people. You have to admire Keynesians and those on the left. They dust themselves off and start all over again as though none of it had happened.

They are after all masters of the economic universe.

20

Masters of the Economic Universe

To act on the belief that we possess the knowledge and power which enable us to shape the process of society entirely to our liking, knowledge which we do not possess, is likely to make us do much harm.

F. A. Hayek (*Pretence of Knowledge*)[58]

The left believes in pipedreams. Part of that belief is expressed as a continuous call to arms to government to solve economic problems. Keynesian economics is a prominent part of this. It is by no means all of it. The left's faith in the economic powers of government goes beyond Keynesian economics. An important insight into this faith and to its widespread infection of the economics profession was provided by an IMF internal staff paper[59] produced shortly after the GFC.

Pipedreams

The IMF paper caused a stir when made public. Most attention was directed to a view in the paper that there might be advantage in increasing the inflation target from around the current two per cent used by most central banks to around four per cent.

While it was couched in "economists-speak", the basic theme of

---
[58] Lecture reprinted in F.A. Hayek, *New Studies in Philosophy, Politics, Economics and the History of Ideas*, Routledge & Kegan Paul, 1978.
[59] *IMF Internal Staff Paper*, "Rethinking Macroeconomic Policy", 10 February 2010.

the paper was simple enough. It was that improved policies needed to be developed to deal with financial and economic downturns. Three propositions for consideration were outlined.

The first, and the one that grabbed most media attention, was that monetary policy should keep more in the tank, as it were, to deal with downturns. Simply put, the idea was that central banks should set higher inflation targets (say 4 to 5 per cent rather than 2 to 3 per cent). In turn, this would keep interest rates higher and therefore give central banks more scope to reduce them when downturns arrived.

The second proposition was broadly consistent with the first but with a fiscal focus. This was that governments should run tighter ships, as it were, when times were good to allow more scope for stimulus measures when times became bad. Allied with this proposition was the potential construction of expenditure and tax mechanisms which would automatically cut in to boost demand when certain recessionary triggers were breached.

The third proposition was the use of financial regulations, as a third arm of macroeconomic policy, to control asset price fluctuations. When particular asset prices grew exuberantly (house prices in the United States for example), then required bank capital and liquidity ratios, or valuation to loan ratios, would be increased to deter lending for the purchase of these assets. This would leave monetary policy to concentrate, as it does now, on controlling goods and services inflation.

Without debating the worth of these measures individually, the one that grabbed the headlines, to fashion monetary policy to keep inflation to 4 to 5 per cent, would be much more difficult to implement than keeping inflation to 2 to 3 per cent. Four to five could easily morph into six and more per cent. Then inflationary expectations might become difficult to control and lead, for example, to industrial unrest and wage break outs. The community is more likely to treat 2 to 3 per cent inflation as no inflation to speak of, than it would 4 to 5 per cent inflation.

The point at issue is the mindset of the IMF and this applies generally to other international agencies (e.g., the OECD) and to Keynesian public sector economists. They all have a view that the economy can and should be controlled and that this will potentially produce better outcomes, if only it is got right. The fact that the GFC occurred, on some measures comparable in its immediate impact to the Great Depression (despite years of practised intervention into economic affairs by governments and their economists) moves them not at all; not one jot. Irony is lost on them. Modesty is a foreign concept. The thought is not that we have contributed to a complete mess with inappropriate intervention and have to reflect on our ability to control economic events. It is that we didn't get it quite right. It's like the take on the Eastern Europe experience by hard-line latter-day socialists. It will work next time, once we have tinkered and ironed out the flaws.

Governments and their economists should understand that the best they can do is to run their own budgetary affairs prudently and otherwise create a stable and predictable background against which the economy can play out, with all of its inevitable (and in large part valuable) ups and downs. They don't. They consider themselves as akin to engineers with machinery, with a similar ability to fine tune.

What makes the authors of the IMF research paper think that people can be found who will be clever enough to keep inflation at 4 to 5 per cent? Or who can develop and orchestrate fiscal automatic stabilisers of appropriate detail, scope and dimension? Or who can intervene in a timely and appropriate way in altering financial regulations as particular asset prices rise and fall? Quite simply, people have never been found so far who are clever enough to do anything like that.

Milton Friedman once observed that governments inevitably get their timing wrong leading to more pronounced economic cycles than would otherwise be the case. Once they start fiddling with monetary, fiscal and regulatory levers, in the way canvassed in the IMF paper, who knows what further damage they would do.

The difficulty with these masters of the universe – governments and their economists – is that each economic downturn, however produced or worsened by inappropriate intervention, simply provides, in their minds, another opportunity to go back to the interventionist drawing board. As the paper says: "Capitalizing on the experience of the crisis, our job will be … to come up with creative policy innovations …". We should say together in loud voices: please don't!

Again, where is King Canute when he is needed? Who will save us from these masters of the universe? They create expectations that simply can't be fulfilled. They have at their disposal a quack (Keynesian) medicine made in 1936. No protestations or cries of anguish from the patient will diminish their ardour to apply it with vigour; and to experiment with variations and enhancements when it fails.

Conclusion

Some people deliver more than they promise. So the story goes, the verdict after a screen test on Fred Astaire was, "Can't sing. Can't act. Balding. Can dance a little." Some deliver far less than they promise.

Interventionist economists and the governments they serve promise much. They deliver very little that isn't counterproductive and damaging. It is all a product of bad economics entirely divorced from the practicalities and realties that good economics takes into account. Resources will always be scarcer than we would like them to be. Needs are endless. The problem is how best to meet them with the resources available. Good economics provides the answer.

The final chapter goes back again to the economic mess that the Western world is in to assess whether there are glimmers of hope, what they are, and how they might be embraced in a grand bargain between conservatives and those on the what can be called the industrial left of the political spectrum.

21

Grand Bargain

Politics is the art of the possible
(Otto von Bismarck, 1867)

Centre stage in 2008 and 2009, the GFC gave way in 2011 to the global (government) debt crisis (GDC) marked by unsustainable budget deficits and government debt, allied with moribund economies and high unemployment. What a complete economic mess. Sarcasm is unbecoming, so let's leave aside how this possibly could have happened when governments and their economists have long had Keynesian tools to give them mastery over economic events. Is there a way out?

Debt and Deficits

As perverse as it sounds the GDC might just turn out to be a good thing. The GFC led to a set of woeful policy responses from governments. Policy responses to the GDC, on the other hand, show promise of pushing back some of the more egregious theories and assumptions that have guided economic and social policy since the 1930s. Maybe the GDC is the economic crisis that had to be had; and, to the extent it has been exacerbated by the policy responses to the GFC, perhaps both crises, fingers crossed, will prove beneficial in the end result. It may take some years to find out.

According to an IMF rule of thumb 60 per cent of GDP is considered an "acceptable" level of public-debt. Some argue that higher levels are sustainable, up to say 90 per cent. It depends on the fiscal position of the country concerned, its rate of economic growth, the level of foreign assets it may have to offset debt and whether contingencies lurk, such as the potential need to bail out banks holding devaluing public debt.

On any measure, the equation is usually stark for countries burdened by government debt at or close to 100 per cent of GDP, and whose economies are moribund with high unemployment. In these circumstances, taxation revenue suffers, welfare expenditure rises, and debt servicing costs eat into revenue. Budget deficits tend to blow out and add more to debt and debt servicing costs. It is a vicious circle; no different from that faced by individuals or businesses which get themselves into similar positions. Once debt rises materially above 100 per cent of GDP, the problem can easily become explosive, particularly if lenders demand higher interest rates to rollover maturing debt or to take on additional debt.

In mid-2011, the OECD projected that gross public debt (measured across all OECD countries) would hit 105 per cent within a year. The United States, Japan, France, Italy, Portugal, Belgium, Ireland, Greece and Iceland all fell across the 100 per cent threshold, some extravagantly so. A number of other counties, including the United Kingdom, were approaching dangerous debt territory. At the same time, government budget deficits, measured across all OECD countries, were projected to be at over 5 per cent; over 9 per cent in the United States. Few governments save anymore. Continued high levels of dissaving (budget deficits) and onerous debt is an explosive combination.

Government debt and deficits are accompanied by moribund economies with high unemployment.[60]. Keynesians should (but don't)

---

60 Unemployment in the United States was 9.1 per cent in mid-2011; in France 9.7%; in Italy 8%; in the UK 7.7 % and in Germany 6.1%. These numbers are high enough, but modest when set against Spain 21% (green jobs notwithstanding); Greece 15%, Ireland 14% and Portugal 12% (OECD, August 2011).

question how high unemployment is possible when public sector spending has bulked so large in the economic affairs of each of the affected countries.

It is sometimes said that countries are not like commercial businesses. There is a difference. Countries don't go out of business; they always remain going concerns. However, like businesses they have often and can default on their debt. And like businesses, and like individuals, once in debt the option of defaulting can only be forestalled by having a rich benefactor, or raising revenue, or cutting costs. Rich benefactors eventually get sick of helping, apropos Germany. This leaves increasing revenue and cutting costs. Increasing revenue is seldom an option for loss-making businesses or for governments presiding over moribund economies. Sure the "rich" can be taxed a bit more. This is superficially attractive but usually brings in less revenue than its proponents expect; and, as I have explained, takes way from private savings which are needed to support investment. Cutting costs is usually the only solution capable of turning the position around.

For governments, cutting costs means spending less, the antithesis of Keynesianism at times of high unemployment. Nevertheless, that is precisely the course set by all governments to combat the GDC. While the aftermath of the GFC showed that Keynesianism doesn't work, the GDC has driven the point home. Fiscal consolidation (the buzz term for reducing budget deficits) and austerity measures have become the new names of the game. Herein lies hope.

Hope from Adversity

The changing stance of the IMF is instructive. The IMF believes in fiscal discipline. It has the role of bailing out indebted governments. However, in January 2008 when the GFC was beginning to bite, its managing director at the time, Dominique Strauss-Kahn, called for stimulus spending at the World Economic Forum in Davos. This apparently surprised some of his fellow panel members, including the then United States' Treasury Secretary Lawrence Summers, who were unused to IMF fiscal largess.

The IMF appeared to have been chastened by experience. For example, in reporting on the outcome of its annual consultation with the United Kingdom in early June 2011, it endorsed fiscal consolidation. This was despite a backdrop of figures from the UK issued earlier, in May, showing unemployment at 7.7 per cent, including significant growth in long-term unemployment (those out of work for twelve months or more). Mind you we have to be careful. There is always backsliding in the offing.

An IMF staff paper[61] prepared for a G20 meeting in mid-October 2011 (to discuss the debt crisis) said among other things:

> Countries with high debt and facing market pressure must press ahead with 'growth-friendly' consolidation now. In others, fiscal policy should navigate between the perils of undermining credibility and undercutting recovery, and facilitate a pickup in private demand.

Described as a key point, this piece of flawed economic advice has the built in advantage of being barely decipherable which may have prevented it from having influence. How it translated into French and German and other languages is hard to know. However, on the whole, it appears to suggest that maybe some countries should do a bit of stimulating amid the austerity of most. To back this up, we are told that the "overarching risk [to growth] is the paradox of thrift as households, firms, and governments around the world reduce demand".

The so-called paradox of thrift received rites of passage into the lexicon of economics through Keynes. It stems from Mandeville's poem "Fable of the Bees" (1705), which describes how a prosperous vibrant community is brought to a sorry state when the inhabitants

---

[61] *IMF Staff Paper*, "Global Economic prospects and Policy Challenges", October 2011.

forswear all luxuries and excesses. It is an insightful concept, unfortunately brought to ruin by a simplistic Keynesian treatment, which is rolled out periodically, as though it had meaning and application in the modern world.

Of course a society that deliberately lived a bare existence would, by definition, be impoverished and, possibly, in a self-afflicted sense, underemployed. There may be some reclusive hair-shirted religious communities who live like this. But for the vast majority of us bare living is not attractive; it is something to be avoided at all costs. We are softies. We prefer five star hotels to leaky tents. Mandeville's fable does not apply to us in the least. Nor for the same reason does Keynesian economics. They particularly and patently do not apply just now when governments and households are heavily over-borrowed. Governments and people alike have shown no sign of wanting to live barely. In Europe, protesters against austerity measures appear not to be objecting to their own extravagant living.

The apparent paradox is that if we all tried to save more, production and employment would fall and savings with them. In fact there is no paradox. The mistake is in assuming, as did Keynes, that capitalist economies default to unemployment when, in fact, they are rife with unsatisfied demands waiting to be filled. Given half a chance entrepreneurs and businesses will attempt to fill them by converting collective savings into investment; always provided government gets out of the way and stays out of the way.

The IMF is giving a mixed message. Its core position is to support fiscal consolidation. Unfortunately, it is also infected with Keynesianism, which keeps breaking out just when we think it's been eradicated. The simple economic message for governments and individuals that have systematically spent more than their incomes is to cut back their spending and save more. This will not send economies into a tailspin as feared by the IMF in its fevered Keynesian moments. What will do that are more wasteful dollops of capricious government expenditure, feckless and unconvincing attempts to rein in budget deficits, and onerous regulations. Get rid of all three and, given a little time, the private sector will roar ahead.

Thankfully the G20 meeting gave the milksop component of the IMF advice short shrift and confirmed the need to cut spending.

It may be a touch optimistic in all of the circumstances but the core stance of the IMF and, more importantly, the preparedness of governments to implement austerity measures when facing unemployment, can, I think, be read as representing the last rites on the body of Keynesian economics. While die-hard faithful Keynesian economists like Paul Davidson, Robert Skidelsky and Paul Krugman will never see it that way, the hard-nosed can spot a dead body when they see it.

Western governments with perhaps the United States coming up behind (not surprising with Obama and Geithner in charge of the economy) have all decided on fiscal consolidation at the same time as having stubbornly high unemployment rates. They now appear to understand at last that Keynesianism does not work. Hopefully that understanding will find increasing expression in universities and in the media.

Making Keynesian economics an historical curiosity is one potential benefit of the GDC. This would allow economies to adjust to changing circumstances and to grow more robustly. As equally important is its potential for substantially rolling back the welfare state.

The size of the debt problem is a product of entitlement spending. It can be solved only by cutting back that spending. In the United States, for example, spending on Medicare, Medicaid and Social Security takes up close to 60 per cent of the federal government's budget and is the fastest growing. Defence takes around 25 per cent. This leaves little scope for deep enough cuts elsewhere. Unaffordable pension and other benefits to public-sector workers across states and municipalities add to the problem. Budgets cannot be brought back to a position to stabilise the level of debt, never mind reduce debt, without material cuts to entitlements. This applies across most Western countries as it does in the United States. Making a start on this in Europe provoked public protests in 2011; more can be expected. Protests can also be expected in the United States. A taste of this was evident in demonstrations and sit-ins in Wisconsin in 2010 when the new Republican governor, with a large state budget deficit to manage, introduced legislation to require public-sector employees to contribute to their own retirement pensions and health insurance and to restrict their collective bargaining rights. The absconding across state lines of fourteen Democrat state senators to prevent a vote on the legislation also highlighted just how partisan politics will complicate the task.

Clearly social dissention on a scale of mass public demonstrations, and perhaps even riots, is deeply concerning. At the same time, there are no easy options. The assumption has to be that democratic institutions across Europe and the United States will be strong enough to withstand the challenge. Leaving this aside, from a purely economic policy perspective, winding down entitlements and, its obverse, winding up self-reliance is an unmitigated good. Self-reliance is an essential building block of capitalism. Capitalism is the only economic system capable of producing prosperity and relieving poverty. It is the only economic system compatible with political freedom. It is worth fighting for and facing up to social dissention.

Governments stripped of their Keynesian illusions and faced with high unemployment and an essential need to cut entitlement spending will be searching for solutions to ease the pain. One clear and evident solution is to reduce artificial barriers to private sector investment and growth. That essentially comes down to reducing and removing regulatory burdens; in other words, cutting red tape and relaxing environmental, financial and workplace regulations and restrictions.

Cutting red tape is the easiest for governments to contemplate; though announced intentions in this area may not be matched by future experience. The trends have been inexorably up.

In a world of green politics and global-warming alarmism, relaxing environmental regulations will be difficult. But it has to be driven home that the use of less efficient forms of energy will impose an additional burden on economies and reduce their ability to go on funding entitlements; even reduced entitlements.

Financial deregulation will also be hard because there have been rounds of increased regulation since the GFC. Hope springs in the United States, as it often does. For example, the Republican Party seems intent on repealing the *Dodd-Frank Wall Street Reform* and *Consumer Protection Act* passed in 2010, if it were to gain the presidency in 2012.

Substantial labour market deregulation will be tough to crack particularly as those on the industrial left (blue collar workers and those representing them in trade unions and in political office) will be needed as allies in any rolling back of environmental obstacles to investment; particularly in Europe.

The potential for relaxing regulation on business lies in the lack of alternatives. Once a government and a society has run down its wealth and created enormous burdens on a proportionately declining number of taxpayers, the alternatives are limited to becoming progressively poorer or to becoming more productive. Freeing business from onerous regulatory barriers is the key to productivity.

The GFC spawned a series of unfortunate and damaging policy responses, just as the economic malaise in the United States in the 1930s led to the New Deal or, to stretch a point, as the economic malaise in Germany in the 1920s contributed to the rise of Nazism. Clearly, economic crises can have unfortunate consequences. The GDC might too, particularly if the need to substantially reduce entitlements results in unmanageable consequences for civil order.

Freeing the private sector to flourish is the least painful way out. The hope has to be that governments will renew their confidence and faith in capitalism, stare down special interests, particularly environmentalists, and take it.

Changing Course

It is often the case that people going down a debilitating path in their personal lives need to experience a crisis before changing course. It is now clear that this applies to nation states. The trends would not have changed of their own volition. Everything that has happened over the past three-quarters of a century pointed to more of the same. The GDC has potentially changed the economic future.

Unsustainable debt and deficits show promising signs of forcing some material reversal of past trends. Keynesianism is now under great scrutiny and threat because those who have followed its precepts find that they are untenable. Killing off Keynesian quackery once and for all, if it were to occur, might also contribute to the forming of a more grounded view of the power of government. The need to replace extravagance with austerity might start to undo some of the more egregious aspects of the nanny state. The competing imperatives of austerity on the one hand and maintaining the welfare state, albeit pared, on the other, might produce some rolling back of regulatory impediments to private sector growth. This is all grasping at straws to a degree.

Good economics points to free market capitalism, smaller government, less intrusive government, deregulation, and more flexible labour markets, as the key to growth and increasing prosperity. In turn, prosperity is the key to having the wherewithal to help those in genuine need. Let us be realistic. This is not achievable in anything approaching full measure in the foreseeable future. What might possibly be achievable is to move closer to the ideal and away from where we are now by striking a compromise or, what might be called, a grand bargain between conservatives and those on the industrial left.

Grand Bargain

The promising policy responses to the GDC provide the basis for a grand bargain between the conservative and industrial left side of politics, and its blue-collar constituency, that could protect the economic future of the West. The key lies in curtailing entitlement spending and some of the more egregious examples of public sector employment largesse while, at the same time, relaxing some of the more onerous regulatory impediments to economic growth.

A first thing to say is that any accords or agreements forged in Europe and in the United States to cap budget deficits will be meaningless and unachievable unless there is entitlement reform. It would be like a team setting out to win a cup final without first putting in the hard yards on the training ground.

Open-ended arrangements for health and pension benefits must be tightened; they are unaffordable under any circumstances. At the same time, it is clear that the nanny state will not be dismantled anytime in the foreseeable future. In fact, the likelihood is that the scope of entitlements will continue to broaden. For example, government subsidisation of child care, of medical care, of dental care, of disability support, of shelter, will continue to occupy the agenda of political parties, particularly, but not exclusively, of the left. In this lies the key to the bargain.

If entitlements cannot be afforded now, how can a broadening of entitlements ever be afforded? A large part of the answer lies in encouraging a vibrant growing free-market capitalist economy. The bargain would differ between countries of course but two essential elements would be common.

First, entitlements of all kinds, including unconditional unemployment benefits and pensions provided by the public sector and government, must be more rigorously ring-fenced and means-tested, albeit in phased-in fashion, if this proves necessary to obtain the necessary support among voting populations. In part, this might mean effectively tearing up and redoing what amounts to contractual obligations. That is precisely what happens after a company goes bankrupt. And it needs to happen now that the public sector and governments are effectively bankrupt. Means-testing benefits should be capable of gaining cross-political support. Conservatives should support the increased emphasis it would place on self-reliance; and those on the left should support the removal of benefits from those able to provide for themselves and the targeting of benefits to those who can't. It would be a balancing act but a way through seems feasible.

Second, regulations imposed on businesses and industry which impair economic development and growth must be significantly wound back. Increases in economic growth and jobs should have cross-political support among conservatives and those on the industrial left. However, this support would not extend to green parties, particularly when it comes to environmental regulations. The environmental lobby would have to be cut adrift and sidelined by those on the industrial left. Onerous environmental regulations and carbon dioxide abatement crush job creation and prosperity. We cannot pay for entitlements from a starting position of penury, if we hamstring industrial development and energy generation. It is simply crazy.

Wherever and whenever you look major projects are held up, whether it is drilling in Arctic waters, or building an oil pipeline from Canada to Texas (Keystone), or building an oil processing plant in Western Australia (James Price Point). At the same time, vast amounts of taxpayers' money are subsidising the generation of inefficient energy. This is not researching "less-polluting" energy sources. This is actually building things to produce energy inefficiently while discarding and dismantling or not developing efficient energy sources. I don't believe that something of this kind has ever happened before. Let us drive ourselves backwards; which is where you don't want to find yourself if you do ever have to deal with effects of global warming. This does not mean doing nothing. It means adopting no regret policies which have their emphasis on progressively improving energy efficiency within measured and phased-in emission standards. It means allowing the market to determine energy forms within those standards; and it means developing policies to deal better with untoward climate events.

Relaxing labour market regulations would be enormously helpful too in creating jobs and reducing unemployment but the scope for agreement here would be limited and would have to be tackled around the edges.

I have said nothing about taxes. Effectively taxation will become a second order issue if governments can reduce their entitlement spending and free the private sector from onerous regulation. A number of principles should guide taxation.

Income taxes, at some level, should be applied to as many people as possible so that as many people as possible understand that government spending has to be paid for. It must also be remembered, and taken into account, that shunting additional taxes on the rich has the cost of reducing saving and investment. The taxation regime should be as simple and straightforward as possible so that it does not create a whole unproductive industry working out how to avoid its impact. Its impact should be as uniform as possible so that it doesn't advantage some businesses or industries over others. Complex taxation regimes with, for example, ranges of different deductions for particular activities, give rise to unintended consequences. No-one can work these out. No-one is clever enough. Certainly the politicians and public servants who put these regimes in place aren't; nor are their computer models. We can't be too modest when it comes to taxation and everything to do with the economy. This, in fact, is the overriding guiding principle.

As to rates of taxation, there is no science. Supply-side theory, popularised in the Reagan era by economist Arthur Laffer, suggests that lowering taxes, by stimulating economic activity, brings in more taxation revenue. Conservatives like this theory. But it is empty. A moment's reflection tells us that 100 per cent taxation, like zero taxation, brings in no revenue. Between zero and 100 per cent, revenue is likely to follow an indeterminate and unstable parabolic curve, rising as taxation rates are increased above zero and falling as rates approach 100 per cent. It follows from this that there will an inflection point on the curve where increasing taxes will bring in less revenue while lowering taxes will bring in more revenue. But, and it is always a big but, no-one has any idea where this shifting point is likely to be and will never know. Modesty, modesty, is required of conservatives as it is of progressives. The overriding objective in the government spending-taxation revenue equation is to get government spending down. All else is secondary.

The economic situation is threatening. Those governments in Europe attempting to bailout or orchestrate the bailout of the perilously positioned are themselves parlously positioned. The United States urges Europe to get its house in order from a position of reckless profligacy. *In the kingdom of the blind, the one-eyed man is king.*

Promise sits alongside threat because the only feasible policy options facing governments are largely confined to those that will be beneficial in the long run. Unemployment and debt have come together to create an economic maelstrom from which there is but one narrow avenue of escape. The question is whether sufficient weight of support can be found among governments, politicians, trade unions and voters to find the way through by embracing good economics. Any alternative course (as I said at the beginning in the Prologue) risks producing social unrest of convulsive proportions and the potential loss of our freedoms.

Appendix: Temperamental Bias

Hypothesis

Dependency on government patronage among businesses and individuals forms a growing constituency. A key to why this is occurring might lie in the evolving temperament of Western societies. Maybe rugged individualism is increasingly giving way to refined collectivism. Hypothetically, perhaps Western societies are becoming less "masculine" and more "feminine" in the way they approach a range of matters, including economic ones.[62]

Commonality of Views

On its face, it is puzzling. You might be having coffee with someone whom you are still getting to know and adventurously venture out of mundane conversation into some news item. Depending on what is said, you will know with a fair degree of certainty that you will either agree about everything of importance or about nothing. There is seldom an in-between.

The question is why conservatives think as they do; and why those on the left think as they do, across a diverse range of subject matters and issues. Is there a common factor that once understood makes sense of the fall of views? Does it matter? I suggest that it does and that it has implications for the scope we have to get back to a sensible economic path.

---

62 See Peter Smith, "The Trumping Factor", *Quadrant*, June Issue, 2010, for a fuller version of this hypothesis.

The geographical context is North America and Western Europe with Australia and New Zealand in the mix. The same reasoning makes (I think) less sense in the rest of the world.

Economics Divide

As a broad generalisation, and without trying to be exhaustive, those on the left tend to have the following economic views.

- Free markets produce chronically unfair outcomes that must be corrected by government intervention to redistribute income and wealth.
- Cyclical downswings must be countered by Keynesian stimulus spending.
- People are entitled to a minimum level of income, adequate shelter, quality education and health services, and now often to help, such as subsidised child-minding services, in raising their children.
- Globalisation has a range of deleterious side-effects on local communities.
- Wealthy nations have a duty to provide substantial aid to poorer nations.

To some extent the demarcation between the views of conservative economists and those on the left is one of degree and emphasis. Nevertheless, it is still easy enough to spot the differences. An economic conservative would want a minimum of intervention and then to improve opportunities rather than to equalise outcomes. An economic conservative would disagree about the worth of stimulus spending; would replace the concept of entitlement with one of aspiration; would point to the benefits of globalisation in increasing prosperity; and would not see foreign aid as an obligation but as a transfer payment from domestic taxpayers, with an attendant need to assess its affordability and effectiveness pragmatically.

This is all familiar territory in the economic sphere. The question is whether there is a similar divide of views across other subject matter and issues which help identify a common factor to make some sense of it all.

Broader Divide

Three subject areas are very briefly and selectively considered: biology, the environment and politics.

A number of well-recognised partisan positions are set out below. While I might have put them in too sharp a relief, the general thrust and character of the different positions is (I think) fairly close to the mark. As in the economic sphere, the issues brought into play are meant to be illustrative not exhaustive.

In the biological sphere those on the left tend to believe that there is no difference of substance, apart from the superficial, between men and women or between different races and cultures. Conservatives, on the other hand, tend to the view that there may be differences which, in some circumstances, may bear on performance.

In the environmental sphere, those on the left are more likely to place a higher value on environmental protection over economic growth than are conservatives. They are more likely to accept and want to counter perceived threats to the environment, such as man-made global warming, without the same regard for costs as conservatives. Consistently, they support the development of green energy and oppose nuclear energy. Conservatives tend to support any form of energy provided it can stand on its own economic feet and meet measured environmental requirements.

In the political sphere, those on the left generally believe that America, and Western civilisation generally, has been exploitative of less developed nations and indigenous populations. Conservatives tend to be more celebratory than critical of their nation's past.

Common Factor

At issue is whether there is a common factor that cuts across different subject areas in a way which makes sense of the dispersion of left-wing and conservative positions, and explains their predictability. There have been recent views that having a conservative or, alternatively, a left-wing orientation might be hard-wired in the brain in some way.[63] Even if there is some measure of validity to this (which I doubt) it still leaves unexplained the predictability of views across quite different areas. After all, why should those who believe in government intervention to modify the outcomes of capitalism necessarily believe in man-made global warming? Why should those who believe in the primacy of free market capitalism be, on the whole, sceptical about man-made global warming? Why should those who passionately advocate using green energy, support making apologies and reparations to indigenous peoples? Why should those who believe that America has done harm also tend to dismiss any idea of performance-related gender and racial differences? Why, in other words, are there only two camps? Why aren't there many camps? As an example, why aren't there lots of economic conservatives belonging to peace movements?

There are a number of potential common-factor candidates: intelligence; socio-economic status; personality; and temperament. As will be shown, the latter candidate, explained and defined in a particular way, seems to offer an answer which better fits the evidence.

It is fairly clear that whatever is the common factor it isn't intelligence. Even though both sides often express exasperation with the other's inability to grasp the point, neither side has, or believes it

---

63 See for example an experiment conducted in 2010 by the University College London which pointed to conservatives having bigger amygdala and thinner anterior cingulates than left-wingers.

has, any measurable edge on intelligence. It is also clear that socio-economic status is not the common factor. Billionaires can be found on either side (for example, billionaire George Soros is very much on the left), as can lawyers, engineers, economists and doctors. Actors and entertainers can't be found much on the conservative side but, then again, the late Charlton Heston's line, that more closet Republicans live in Hollywood than closet gays, bears thinking about. While the media and academia tend to be on the left, conservatives are managing to fight a rearguard action to retain some material presence.

Personality might come into it. On examination this seems unlikely. There are many variants of personality scales. However the "big five [personality] factors" used in psychology are openness, conscientiousness, extraversion, agreeableness, and neuroticism, each contrasted with its opposite.[64] There is some evidence that those on the left tend to be more open than conservatives and more likely to embrace what is new, as you would expect. Conservatives quite clearly are more suspicious and cautious about change. However, this seems to explain little as distinct from simply putting an alternative badge on those on the left and conservatives. None of the other personality factors have been shown to be systematically associated with political leanings.[65] This leaves temperament.

Social welfare entitlements have grown rapidly in scope and size since the end of the Second World War. Providing people with entitlements might be considered to be a nurturing and protective thing to do. Let me take a leap: this appears to be quintessentially feminine in its orientation. In turn, the growth of the nanny state and a culture of entitlement are also quintessentially part of the agenda of those on the left. There appears to be a coincidence worth exploring.

---

64 See, for example, *Handbook of Personality*, O.P. John, R.W. Robins and L.A. Pervin, The Guilford Press, 2008.
65 See G. Giavittorio and M. Vecchione, "Personality and Politics", *The Cambridge Handbook of Personality Psychology*, edited by P.J. Corr and G. Mathews, CUP, 2009.

There is a view that Western society is becoming more feminised. Google "the feminisation of society" and get many hundreds of thousands of references. Google "the masculinisation of society" and get far fewer and many of them are about physiology rather than sociology. Two articles in the Australian conservative magazine *Quadrant* provide some insight into this phenomenon. Patrick McCauley in the September 2008 issue wrote that for some years, "Australian Rules football has been in the hands of feminine social engineers who wish to establish equity and social justice in the football community". Taken from a Veterans' Day address to staff and students of the US Marine Corps,[66] Michael Evans, in the January-February 2010 issue, commented that "radical feminism" is one of a number of developments since the 1960s representing the "greatest challenge to the Western profession of arms".

A culture of entitlement, sport, and the military spans a wide area suggesting that the potential influence of a feminine temperamental bias may be far-reaching. The question arises as to whether a feminine-masculine temperamental divide could be the common factor influencing the fall of views between those on the left and conservatives.

First, it is necessary to think of feminism and masculinism in rather different ways than the obvious. Prime Minister Clement Atlee, who gave the United Kingdom its welfare state, and President Roosevelt, who through the New Deal started the process in the United States, hardly epitomised femininity (at least to my mind).

A sociological paper by Stets and Burke throws light on the issue.[67] In that paper the feminine temperament in Western culture is characterised as being "passive, cooperative, and expressive" and the masculine temperament as being "aggressive, competitive, and

---

[66] University at Quantico Virginia, November 2009.

[67] J.E. Stets & P.J. Burke, "Femininity/Masculinity", *Encyclopedia of Sociology*, Macmillan, 2000.

instrumental". While this precise categorisation is not universally followed across the sociology literature, it is broadly in sync with other categorisations. Accordingly, it is reasonable to use it as the benchmark in assessing whether a feminine-masculine (F-M) divide might be the common factor.

It is important to understand that the feminine and masculine characteristics of temperament (a person's nature as it affects their behaviour) cut across women and men, even if gender has some influence. Passivity and aggression, for example, form part of both men's and women's temperament. Any difficulty with this can be despatched by comparing the on-show temperaments of Margaret Thatcher ("You turn if you want to. The lady's not for turning.") and Jimmy Carter.

The meanings of passive and aggressive are fairly self-evident, as are the meanings of cooperative and competitive. The meanings of expressive and instrumental are less obvious. In this context, expressive means socialisation with others (arising out of say affection or kinship) as an end in itself. Instrumental means socialisation purposefully pursued, taking account of costs and consequences, in order to achieve practical goals.

Economic Sphere

The economic positioning of those on the left and of conservatives exhibits a pattern which is consistent with the F-M divide. The Left's position is characterised by a lack of calculation. The overriding objective is one of showing commitment to others (expressive). That is the be-all and end-all. The conservative position on the other hand is goal-oriented and full of calculation (instrumental). Will stimulus spending actually work? Can those entitlements be afforded? Do the benefits of globalisation outweigh the costs?

A lot falls into place when the economic divide is put in context of the expressive-instrumental divide. It is why those on the left can think conservatives lack empathy and why conservatives can get exasperated with those on the left who celebrate yet another new entitlement without too much obvious regard to its cost and achievability.

The other components of the F-M divide: passive-aggressive and cooperative-competitive, also have explanatory powers in the economics area. Capitalism is underscored by a determined and energetic (aggressive) pursuit of profit and reward. It is competitive in its nature. It is understandable that those with a passive and cooperative temperament would favour intervention to moderate the outcomes that capitalism produces; built as it is around aggression and competition.

Broader Spheres

The F-M divide appears to retain its explanatory power in the biological sphere, specifically on whether performance can be affected by gender or racial/cultural differences. The emphasis on performance is the key. Those whose temperament is weighted towards being instrumental, competitive, and aggressive will very much focus on performance. Consequently, they will have an imperative to discover and identify performance-affecting differences, if they exist. However, those whose temperament is weighted towards being expressive, cooperative, and passive will not focus so much on performance and therefore on such differences. Among other things, this makes sense of support for affirmative action on the part of those on the left.

Affirmative action is based on the view that any under representation of particular groups, in particular occupations, is because of environmental factors, rather than because of innate differences in abilities. If that is the case, affirmative action makes more sense than it does if there are in fact innate differences. Conservatives do not rule out the possibility of there being innate differences. Though saying so, whoever you are, and whatever your political leanings, can be problematic. Then Harvard president Lawrence Summers (hardly on the conservative side) suggested at a conference about women in science in 2005 that there may be innate differences between men and women in their aptitude for the hard sciences. Universities these days are not the place for such views on touchy biological matters, as shortly thereafter ex-president Summers discovered.

At first glance, it is not immediately obvious that the environmental divide can be explained by the F-M divide. After all, environmentalists are not particularly passive in pursuing their objectives. Nevertheless, the lack of attention to the achievability and costs of proposals put forward by environmentalists, for example, on moving to green energy or in combating global warming, has the hallmark of an expressive temperament. Moreover, the actions taken by environmental zealots often have a Mahatma Gandhi quality about them; being chained to a tree and lying in front of bulldozers, come to mind. Environmentalism also can be seen as cooperative action opposing an individualistic and competitive credo – capitalism – which puts economic advancement ahead of the interests of the planet. All in all, the F-M divide does a fairly decent job of explaining the environmental divide.

The political divide covers a wide canvass. One of the major themes is a view about Western civilisation's military and economic dominance, and how it was achieved. Dominance is only ever achieved through being purposeful (instrumental), determined and energetic (aggressive) and competitive. It is understandable therefore that the outcome of this process is celebrated by conservatives (who are in sync with it) and regarded with an amount of distaste by those whose temperament is largely governed by polar opposite characteristics. Nor is it surprising that the epitome of dominance, the United States, is regarded with particular odium by those on the left. This also explains the Left's empathy with those whom it regards as victims of the process: indigenous populations and Third World countries who continue to suffer at the hands of the "rapacious" West. It explains the phenomenon of national self-loathing, which conservatives have particular difficulty in comprehending, as a logical outcome of despising the process that put Western nations (whether the United States, the United Kingdom, Australia or some other Western nation) at the top of the economic pile.

Positions on immigration and refugees provide another example in the political sphere. An expressive, cooperative, and passive temperament does not focus on costs nor on threats to social cohesion. Conservatives, with their polar opposite temperaments, precisely focus on costs and threats.

On disarmament and peace, an expressive, cooperative, and passive temperament always searches for a negotiated outcome. Conservative Republicans were extremely sceptical and scathing of proposals by President Obama to negotiate with Kim Jong-il and Mahmoud Ahmadinejad during the early part of his presidency. They implicitly knew, whether they acknowledged it or not, that Kim Jong-il and Ahmadinejad were like them, mainly instrumental, aggressive, and competitive; and that appeasement would not work. As Ronald Reagan put it: "If history teaches us anything; it teaches: simple minded appeasement or wishful thinking about our adversaries is folly; it means the betrayal of our past, the squandering of our freedom." In searching for a negotiated outcome, however unlikely its success, President Obama appeared to be governed by an opposite temperament to that of President Reagan. It is hard to understand his actions against the lessons of history unless that is factored in.

Conclusion

It is persuasive, though of course far from conclusive, that the economic divide between conservatives and those on the left is at least partially down to a temperamental divide. It is reasonably clear that the temperament of those on the left is weighted more towards being expressive, cooperative, and passive than it is to being instrumental, competitive, and aggressive. The temperament of conservatives is weighted in the opposite direction. This explains why left-wing and conservative views fall predictably along "party lines" across a range of subject matter. It may partly explain why the two sides exasperate each other in reaching quite different conclusions based on the same information and evidence.

Where does all this lead? A point to make is that one kind of temperament is not better than the other. Individuals and societies need to have a balance of feminine and masculine temperaments. To paraphrase *Ecclesiastes*, there is a time for being expressive and a time for being instrumental; for being passive and for being aggressive; and for being cooperative and for being competitive. A society predominantly masculine in its temperament would tend to be uncaring and prone to economic and military conflict. One predominantly feminine would tend to pursue impractical visions and be susceptible to economic and military subjugation. Neither is appealing. Balance is the key. Unfortunately a number of trends suggest that the balance is skewed. The temperament of Western societies appears to be becoming progressively more feminised and, as an offshoot of this, more inclined to embrace bad economics and other left-wing baggage.

While it is contentious to say that this or that societal balance of feminine-masculine temperament is skewed, sometimes the evidence speaks for itself. Entitlements and the promise of entitlements are everywhere growing, even though most governments outspend their revenue and are heavily in debt. Green political parties are gaining increasing support, even though the implementation of their policies would cause impoverishment. There is widespread support for disruptive, expensive and ineffective policies to counter an unproven climate threat. Nuclear power and (on and off-shore) drilling for oil is often resisted and disallowed because it risks causing environmental harm. Affirmative action is an accepted part of public sector employment policy. Western governments acquiesce to large inflows of displaced people and refugees, even though the numbers involved are clearly straining social cohesion and budgets. Apologies to indigenous populations are de rigueur whatever the rights and wrongs. Military action now almost invariably results in trenchant media criticism and what, in an early age, would have been called defeatism.

President Obama committed the United States not to use nuclear weapons against a non-nuclear state that is a signatory to the non-proliferation treaty, even if the United States is attacked with chemical or biological weapons. In making this commitment, the President reportedly removed ambiguity about the United States' nuclear policy. Having a quite different temperament, President Reagan no doubt saw advantage in ambiguity to confound and confuse potential enemies.

Accepting the premise, it is difficult to say why Western society is becoming more feminised. Sociologists are insistent that temperament is not hard-wired, but learnt. This certainly accords with common sense. It seems unlikely that relatively more people are now being born with a left-temperament bias. An iterative process may be involved with the entitlement society engendering dependency which, in turn, engenders claims for more entitlements, rather like an addiction. Being protected and cared for is appealing. In the animal kingdom, as in the human kingdom, parents often have to push the young away to fend for themselves. The offer of protection for life under the care of government – from parental embrace to government embrace – is a powerful siren call.

Other factors might also be at work: for example, the dramatic shifts that have occurred in employment in Western economies in recent decades away from manual work towards services and government employment. Or, the rise of the feminist and gay rights movements (however worthy). Or, the increasing predominance of women in childhood education. Or, the social interaction generated by the extravagant use of texting on mobile phones among young people, or through social networks like Twitter, Facebook and MySpace, exceeding any need for (instrumental) communication by an extremely large factor. It is simply difficult to know. Researching the issue further might provide fertile ground for cooperation between psychologists, sociologists and economists.

Index

Adam, Stuart, 141
Adding up problem, 191, 193–195
Aggregate demand, 31–35, 44, 52, 54-55, 57, 119
American Insurance Group, 93
Astaire, Fred, 200
Atlee, Clement, 220
Austerity measures, 203, 205–206
Australian Bureau of Statistics, 153
Australian Rules football, 220
Austrian economists, 66, 77, 111
Austrian school, 66

Baldwin, Alec, 144
Bank of America, 100
Baqir, Fayyaz, 173
Belafonte, Harry, 150
Bernanke, Ben, 88
Bild, 171
Bismarck, Otto von, 201
Botton, Alain De, 7
Brewer, Mike, 141
British Labour Party, 7, 165
Buffett, Warren, 149–150
Burke, P.J., 220
Bush, George H.W., 61

Caldwell, Christopher, 179
Capitalism, 1–4, 9, 26, 43, 77, 80, 82–83, 87–88, 90, 96–97, 101–103, 110–111, 132, 136, 156, 159–161, 189, 207, 209, 218, 222–223
Cargo cult, 164–166

Castles, Stephen, 179
Chinese Yuan, 91
Chomsky, Noam, 184
Churchill, Winston, 141, 189
Civitas, 171
Classical economics, 36, 39, 42, 48, 50, 52, 56, 60, 66
Classical economists, 34, 39–42, 47, 51, 53, 56, 65, 85–86, 155
Clinton, Bill, 54, 61, 90, 190
Club of Rome, 134
CNN, 54
Communism, 136, 150
Community Reinvestment Act, 89, 96, 128, 130
Comparative advantage, 178–180
Conservative economists, 119, 150, 195, 216
Conservatives, 5, 9, 76, 127, 183–185, 195, 200, 209, 211, 213, 215, 217–225
Conventional wisdom, 34–36, 57, 103, 107, 110, 118–119
Coolidge, Calvin, 157, 164
Corr, P.J., 219
Crackpot, 4, 28, 42–44, 112
Crafts, N.F.R., 177
Creative destruction, 77
Credit default swaps, 93
Crowding out, 43, 69–71, 168
Currency debasement, 63, 66, 91, 111

Darwinism, 159
Davidson, Paul, 80, 206

Davidson, Sinclair, 140
Deuteronomy, 144
Dickens, Charles, 97
Dismal science, 47, 158
Disraeli, Benjamin, 113
Distribution of income, 5, 163
Dodd-Frank, 208
Douglas, Michael, 33

Eastern Europe, 1, 21, 41, 151, 163, 172, 189, 199
Eastwood, Clint, 16
Ecclesiastes, 225
Econometrica, 34, 58
Economic cycles, 4, 27, 36–37, 60–61, 66, 77–79, 199
Economies of scale, 177
Effective demand, 32, 39, 47, 53, 56–57
Einstein, Albert, 48, 107, 174
Environmentalism, 223
Equilibrium, 25, 39, 42, 56
Euler's Theorem, 193
European Union, 178
Evans, Michael, 220

Fannie Mae, 73, 89, 96
Fed funds rate, 91, 95
Federal Reserve, 79, 88, 91, 100
Feminine, 215, 219–221, 225
Findlay, Robert, 176
Fiscal consolidation, 108, 203–206
Fisher, Irving, 83
Ford, Henry, 24
Forward market, 135
Fox News, 143, 149
Framework Convention on Climate Change, 173

Freddie Mac, 73, 89, 96
Friedman, Milton, 30, 75, 100, 199
Frish, Ragnur, 34
Frost, Robert, 165

G20, 78, 106–107, 204, 206
Galbraith, J.K., 35–36, 107–108
Garnaut, Ross, 88, 95
Gates, Bill, 24, 82, 149–150
GATT, 178
GDP, 113–115, 118, 168, 170, 174, 193, 201–202
Geithner, Timothy, 105, 108, 206
Gandhi, Mahatma, 223
Giavittorio, G., 219
Gillard, Julia, 73
Global Debt Crisis, 5
Global Financial Crisis, 4, 30, 41
Good economics, 1, 5, 75, 103, 120–121, 137, 148, 164, 171, 181, 188, 200, 209, 213
Google, 220
Government debt, 1, 32, 69, 73, 76, 85, 101, 108, 133, 171, 201–202
Great Depression, 26, 29, 37–38, 51, 75, 81, 83, 86, 96, 100, 111–112, 116, 199
Green Climate Fund, 174
Greenspan, Alan, 79
Greenwald, Bruce, 177–178

H.M. Revenue & Customs, 153
Hackman, Gene, 16
Harcourt, Geoffrey, 122
Hawke, R.J., 183
Hayek, F.A., 15, 66, 111, 121–122, 197
Health care, 87, 168–169, 184, 188–190
Health insurance, 168, 185, 207

Henry, Ken, 106
Heston, Charlton, 219
Hicks, John, 58
Hoover, Herbert, 51
Hopkins, Anthony, 144–145
Howard, John, 141

IMF, 29, 78, 80, 197, 199, 201, 203–206
Interest rates, 27, 30, 38, 41, 58, 62–63, 65, 67–71, 73, 76, 81, 91, 94, 111, 198, 202
Internal Revenue Service, 140

James Price Point, 211
Joe the plumber, 139
John, O.P., 219

Kahn, Judd, 177–178
Kahn, R.F., 115
Kates, Steven, 47, 110
Kelvin, Lord, 83
Keynes, John Maynard, 1, 3-4, 10, 26-34, 36-44, 47–48, 50-53, 55-58, 65, 68, 80-86, 99, 106–107, 112, 115, 132, 145-146, 204–205
Keynesian economics, 2–5, 11, 29–30, 34, 36, 45, 47–48, 68, 75, 77, 80, 103, 107, 197, 205–206
Keynesianism, 4–5, 29–31, 33–34, 36, 39, 42, 44–45, 55–56, 60–61, 68, 78, 80, 82, 85, 97, 106–110, 118–120, 155, 203, 205–206, 209
Keystone, 211
Kim Jong-il, 224
King Canute, 170, 200
King, Martin Luther, 187
Korten, David, 87
Krugman, Paul, 54–55, 68, 80–81, 105, 107–108, 112, 122, 206

Laffer, Arthur, 30, 213
Lehman Brothers, 101
Leviticus, 144
Liquidity trap, 41
Logan, David S., 140
Luke, 144

Macroeconomics, 34–35, 85, 106–107, 110, 133
Mahmoud Ahmadinejad, 224
Malthus, Thomas, 47–48, 158
Mandeville, Bernard, 204–205
March of events, 36, 103, 107–110, 118–119
Marginal efficiency of capital, 83
Marshall, Alfred, 11, 34, 37, 48
Marx, Karl, 136
Masculine, 215, 220–221, 225
Matthew, 60, 144
Mathews, G., 219
McCauley, Patrick, 220
McGimpsey, Michael, 167
McPherson, Elle, 144
Medicaid, 206
Medicare, 206
Menger, Carl, 66
Micawber, Mr, 97
Microeconomics, 34, 106–107, 133–134
Mill (John Stuart), 23, 34, 37, 48-51, 53
Miller, Mark, 179
Mises, Ludwig, 111
Moch, L.P., 178
Monetarism, 30
Monetary policy, 63, 66, 76, 79, 86, 91–92, 95–96, 198
Money illusion, 8, 149–152

Moore, Michael, 149–150, 161, 184
Moore, Stephen, 54
More, Sir Thomas, 188
Muth, John, 30
Multiplier, 115

Nanny state, 1, 155, 209–210, 219
National accounts, 32, 110, 113–115, 119–120
National Public Radio, 54, 68
Nazism, 208
Neo-classical economists, 85
Neo-liberalism, 97, 131
New Deal, 1, 51, 74–75, 112, 208, 220
New York Times, 105, 107, 111
Newton, Isaac, 48
Nixon, Richard, 30, 55

Obama, Barack, 73–74, 83, 87, 93, 99, 118, 139, 142-143, 145, 150, 152, 165, 168, 185, 189–190, 206, 224, 226
Occupy Wall Street (OWS), 139, 150-151
OECD, 29, 34, 84–85, 170, 193, 199, 202
Orwell, George, 86, 122, 194
Orwellian, 122, 194

Paradox of thrift, 204
Penn, Sean, 150
Pervin, L.A., 219
Philanthropy, 154, 161
Pierson, Paul, 97
Pigou, A.C., 34
Pilger, John, 184
Presley, Elvis, 8
Price inflation, 30, 59, 62-63, 65, 91, 111, 197-199
Price mechanism, 62, 65, 133, 135
Progressive(s), 1, 3, 5, 9, 87, 90, 97, 181, 195, 213
Progressive taxation, 144, 154
Protests, 207
Public debt, 70, 107, 201–202

Quadrant, 215, 220

Rating agencies, 89, 131
Rational expectations, 30
Raz, Guy, 54
Reagan, Ronald, 97, 190, 213, 224, 226
Real interest rates, 65, 111
Red tape, 75, 207–208
Regulation, 60, 75, 80, 99, 101, 127–132, 198–199, 206–209, 211–212
Reich, Robert, 54
Reinhart, C.M., 51, 94, 96
Republican Party, 208
Reserve Bank of Australia, 73
Ricardian, 176
Ricardo, David, 48, 53, 175–177, 179–180
Rizzo, Suzanne, 95
Robins, R.W., 219
Robinson, Joan, 10, 122–123
Rogoff, K.S., 51, 94, 96
Romans, 157
Romer, Christina, 117
Roosevelt, F.D., 1, 51, 74–75, 220
Rudd, Kevin, 73, 87
Russell, Bertrand, 47

Samuelson, Paul, 11
Saunders, Peter, 171
Say (Jean-Baptiste), 39, 47-48, 51, 53
Say's Law, 39, 47, 52, 110
Schumpeter, Joseph, 66, 77
Schwartz, Anna, 100

Second World War, 4, 37, 74, 97, 166, 174, 178–179, 219
Shaw, George Bernard, 37
Shlaes, Amity, 51, 157
Skidelsky, Robert, 80, 85, 206
Smith, Adam, 34, 37, 99, 137, 142, 145–147, 150, 152, 155
Smith, Peter, 215
Social Security, 166, 206
Socialism, 1, 4, 18, 41, 43–44, 110, 120–121, 123, 132, 134, 137, 161, 163, 189
Socialist(s), 9, 16, 80, 81, 87, 97, 121–123, 125–128, 131–137, 148, 161, 195, 199
Socrates, 7, 29
Soros, George, 219
St. Paul, 157
Stets, J.E., 220
Stevens, Glen, 70
Stiglitz, Joseph E., 122
Stimulus spending, 30, 43, 54-55, 67–70, 72–75, 77, 81, 85, 99, 102–103, 105-106, 108, 114–118, 132–133, 165, 198, 203, 216, 221
Strauss-Kahn, Dominique, 78, 203
Sub-prime mortgage crisis, 41
Summers, Lawrence, 204, 223
Supply-side theory, 30, 213

Taleb, Nassim Nicholas, 94
Tammany Hall, 147
Tariff, 178–179
Tea Party, 171
Tech Wreck, 62, 73, 91
Thatcher, Margaret, 97, 187, 221
The General Theory, 26, 29, 31-32, 34, 38, 42–44, 47, 55–56, 58, 81, 83–84, 112, 146
The Monthly, 87
The Wall Street Journal, 54
The Worldwide Fund for Nature, 134
Tithing, 144
Tocqueville, Alexis de, 145
Trump, Donald, 143
Turner, Graham, 86
Turner, Kathleen, 33

Unemployment, 1, 26–28, 30–31, 33, 38–39, 41–42, 44, 47, 54–55, 73–76, 82, 103, 108, 118, 201–207, 210, 212–213
Unforgiven, 16
United Nations General Assembly, 78
University College London, 218
US Marine Corps, 220
Utopia, 185, 187–191
Utopian, 5, 158, 168–169, 181, 189, 191

Vecchione, M., 219

Wall Street, 87, 99
Wantok system, 139
Washington Post, 111
White House Council of Economic Affairs, 117
Wilde, Oscar, 15
Wilson, Harold, 12
Wilson, Sammy, 167
Wolff, Edward, 153
Woods (Thomas E.), 66, 110-162
Wordsworth, William, 79

www.ingramcontent.com/pod-product-compliance
Ingram Content Group UK Ltd.
Pitfield, Milton Keynes, MK11 3LW, UK
UKHW041302180426
11947UKWH00009B/632